OUR SUN-GOD
CHRISTIANITY BEFORE CHRIST

A DEMONSTRATION THAT, THE FATHERS ADMITTED,
OUR RELIGION EXISTED BEFORE OUR ERA, AND
EVEN IN PRE-HISTORIC TIMES

BY

JOHN DENHAM PARSONS

THE BOOK TREE
San Diego, California

First published
1895
by the Author

New material, revisions and cover
© 2007
The Book Tree

ISBN 978-1-58509-297-0

Cover layout and design
by Toni Villalas

Published by
The Book Tree
P.O. Box 16476
San Diego, CA 92176
www.thebooktree.com

We provide fascinating and educational products to help awaken the public to new ideas and
information that would not be available otherwise.
Call 1 (800) 700-8733 for our *FREE BOOK TREE CATALOG*.

INTRODUCTION

Many would dismiss the idea of Christianity before Christ as being ridiculous and would have no willingness to look at any evidence. Yet some church fathers have admitted that the Christian religion did in fact exist before the Christian era, including St. Augustine himself who said, "The very thing which is now called the Christian religion existed among the ancients also, nor was it wanting from the inception of the human race until the coming of Christ in the flesh, at which point the true religion which was already in existence began to be called Christian." This is an extremely important and accurate book for those who are interested enough to look at valid research. It is not for those who are steadfast in saying, "Don't bother me with the facts, I have my beliefs." It approaches the subject from a general church view and a Gnostic point of view, plus chapters on The Hebrew Scriptures, Non-Jewish Evidence, The Sun-God of the New Testament, and Sun-God Worship in the Days of the Fathers. It seems that a man named Jesus may still have existed, but a number of pagan mythologies, those being almost entirely sun-worship components, may have been added or incorporated into the story of his life in order to bring the more stubborn pagans of the time into the Christian fold. This timeless story, of great value to the world throughout time, should not denigrate or diminish Christianity, but should enhance it with a deeper spiritual value for those willing to shed a strict dogmatic viewpoint. It can be difficult to understand what's truly behind our older religions because of their age and the changes that occur over time, but this book goes far in going back to uncover some of the more interesting elements that are shown to exist. This work fits well for us in the modern world, as we continue to gain a better understanding of ourselves and the origins of our beliefs.

Paul Tice

CONTENTS

v

OUR SUN-GOD.

Part I.

FROM A BROAD CHURCH POINT OF VIEW.

CHAPTER I.

PAULINE CHRISTIANITY.

NINETEEN centuries have rolled away since, according to our creed as Christians, the angels of heaven proclaimed to men of earth the Gospel—*i.e.*, the Glad Tidings—of the advent of Jesus. More than eighteen hundred years have passed since the Jewish artisan whom we declare to have been God incarnate, leaving the carpenter's workshop, tried to reform His fellow-countrymen by declaring to them that the final Day of Judgment was at hand. One millennium

2 *OUR SUN-GOD*

has slowly but for ever gone, and even a second millennium has nearly passed away, since the poor Communist of Galilee, whose followers had "all things in common," solemnly affirmed, "Ye cannot serve God and Private-property." At least a hundred generations have one after the other suffered and passed on into the darkness since the followers of Paul were at Antioch first called Christians. And over a millennium and a half divide us from the time when Constantine, the worshipper of the Sun-God Apollo, made the faith so zealously preached by Paul the State Religion of the almost world-wide Roman Empire.

Thanks primarily to the action of Constantine, the Church we belong to had for at least a thousand years the nations of Christendom at its feet, and the almost almighty power of education in its hands. For several centuries, too, it had sole control of the literary records of the wisdom and history of the past, and could destroy or alter what it chose.

It is, alas! greatly to be feared that our Church at times somewhat abused the power in question.

One of the greatest sins against humanity

in the direction indicated was undoubtedly the destruction of the priceless manuscripts which, when Constantine the Great died, were still stored in the famous library of Alexandria.

Upon the strength of an accusation made by a Christian Bishop against the Saracen who conquered Alexandria A.C. 640, this crime has long been charged to the account of the broad-minded and tolerant Caliph Omar, whose behaviour when he captured Jerusalem puts that of the Crusaders to shame. But it is now more or less generally admitted that the invaluable records in question were destroyed at the request of the Christian Bishop of Alexandria some fifty years after the death of Constantine, and two hundred and fifty years before the army of Omar appeared upon the scene.

Yet, notwithstanding such unscrupulous actions as the one referred to seems to have been, notwithstanding the great lapse of time since Paul started its career as a supposed world-conquering force, notwithstanding the unexampled chances and unequalled opportunities which it inherited as a result of succeeding in its youth to the position of State Religion of the world-wide Roman Empire, notwithstanding the fact that the races over which it has had control have been the most strenuous upon the face of the earth, notwithstanding the dying-out before its advancing armies and colonists of many a pagan race,—notwithstanding all these things the Christian Faith has come to a dead halt. For every genuine recruit it obtains otherwise than from the nurseries of its followers, two of its rank and file at heart waver in their allegiance.

As a matter of fact, our faith as Christians, despite the noble efforts of individuals, is, as a whole, losing ground. Not only has Christianity, with all its advantages, failed, even in eighteen centuries, to secure even the nominal suffrages of one half—much less of the whole—of human kind, but the proportion which those who honestly believe in its distinguishing dogmas bear to the remainder of our race, is undoubtedly decreasing.

As a son of the Church, and one convinced of its immense potentialities for good, the author has searched for, and, as he thinks, has found, those weak points in the Christianity of the last eighteen centuries which its history and the present state of affairs betoken.

But the discussion of those weak points does not lie within the province of the present volume, and must be reserved for a future one.

For before the weak points of any one's religion, whatever religion it be, can be anything like accurately gauged, a painful process has to be gone through. So absolutely one-sided in their views are nine hundred and ninety-nine people out of a thousand, and so prejudiced are they in favour of such belief as their education and environment have caused to be their second nature, so few even of the few really earnest ones seek Truth, whatever it may cost, rather than a confirmation of their own opinions, that a necessary preliminary to a just discussion and appreciation of the weak points of one's religion is a personal and searching inquiry into the evidence which can be produced against one's creed.

The greater part of the real or supposed evidence against our creed as Christians, which opponents of Christianity have at one time or another brought forward against us, can be ascertained by an intelligent inquirer without very great difficulty. But the evidence producible by those who believe that the Sun-God worship once prevalent throughout the Roman Empire, did not exactly die out, but became merged or evolved into what is now called Christianity, cannot be so ascertained, and a clear statement of it does not exist. The present volume is therefore an attempt to supply what, if not a want, is, at any rate, a deficiency.

As a conclusion to this introductory chapter, the author would ask the reader, when considering that part of his work written from a Gnostic point of view, to bear in mind (1) that in ancient days religions were national; (2) that the Romans tolerated the religion of every nation they conquered; (3) that their persecution of our faith when it was in its infancy was due to the fact that it was non-national, and therefore from their point of view a hateful superstition undermining the religions of all the nations they protected, and subversive of all good rule; (4) that it was probably the first faith ever preached as intended for all nations; (5) that the Gospels "according to" Matthew, Mark, Luke, and John, were written after Paul went about preaching his new and non-national creed, as it is clear that he was ignorant of all save one of the many great marvels recorded therein,—the miraculous birth and ascension of Jesus, for instance, not being once mentioned in his arguments; (6) that while Paul was by his own confession "all things to all men," Jesus spent much of His time in denouncing the possession of Private-property; (7) that the followers of Jesus had "all things in common"; (8) that it was the followers of Paul who were called Christians; (9) that while Jesus said, "The Scribes and Pharisees sit in Moses' seat: all therefore whatsoever they bid you observe, that observe and do" (Matt. xxiii. 3), Paul was an apostate as regards Judaism; and (10) that Jesus repeatedly declared that His mission was to, and his "gospel" or "glad tidings" for, the Jews alone.

Part II.

FROM A GNOSTIC POINT OF VIEW.

CHAPTER II.

CHRISTIANITY IN EXISTENCE BEFORE CHRIST.

ARCHBISHOP WHATELY has told us that "Not to undeceive, is to deceive"; that "We must neither lead, nor leave, men to mistake falsehood for truth"; and that "He who propagates delusion, and he who connives at it when already existing, both alike tamper with the truth."[1]

These sayings are quite as applicable to our religious teachers as to our teachers of science and philosophy.

---

[1] Archbishop Whately, *On the Essays of Francis Bacon.*

Let us, for instance, see how matters stand as to what they have taught us concerning the origin of our religion.

If Christians—whether followers of the Greek Church (which, as more or less representative of the primitive Church, essentially a Greek one, sometimes claims to be the Mother Church), or followers of that Church which has succeeded to the priestly powers of the Cæsars (and may perhaps be allowed to have the best claim to the title "Catholic"), or followers of the Protestant Churches—if a number of representative Christians were asked the plain question, " Did Christianity exist before the birth of Jesus the Nazarene ? " their answers would be found ultimately divisible into three classes: (1) that of the Christians unable to give a plain and straightforward reply; (2) that of those who would reply "Of course it did not "; and (3) that of those who would reply "Of course it did."

Those who would not give a plain and straightforward answer need not be considered. Those who would give the reply "Of course it did not," would give the only plain answer logically

possible upon the part of those who stand by the
Christian creed as nowadays generally taught.
But the few, the very few, who would answer,
"Of course it did," would have very good
grounds for their assertion.

Some Christians think that even Civilisation
came into the world after, and as a result of, the
advent of Jesus. As a matter of fact, however,
a high state of civilisation existed, in various
countries at various times, thousands of years
before our era. And as to the Roman Empire and
the countries into which that "world in itself" was
ultimately split up, it is well known that as Christianity triumphed so Civilisation died out. Whatever may have been the cause, none can deny
the fact that the Dark Ages followed close in the
wake of the conquering Church.

It is true that the Monks were for centuries
the centres of such light and learning as survived
in Europe. And why was this ? It was because
Constantine the Great having utilised his power,
as High Priest of the Gods of Rome and supreme
Emperor of the whole Roman world, in favour of
Christianity, making it the State Religion, the

Christian Church became mistress of the situation, and got Emperor after Emperor not only to increase its power, but also to stamp out of existence the literary evidence against its own version of the nature, origin, and history of the Christian Faith; the Church itself taking possession of all the manuscripts which were to be saved, and, by securing a monopoly of the power to educate, thus safeguarding and perpetuating its powers and privileges.

As to the contention that our present civilisation is due to the monks and to Christianity, it is more than fifteen hundred years since the Sun-God worshipper Constantine laid the whole Roman world at the feet of the Christian Church, and also gave it a monopoly of the right to benefit by endowment; a right still refused to its opponents even in free England. It was in the first half of the fourth century of our era that Christianity was made the state religion of the Roman Empire, let us look a century ahead of the date in question, and ask ourselves whether the Christian Church had been employing its immense powers in favour of science and of

progress ?   Was the state of Christendom in the
sixth, seventh, eighth, ninth, tenth, eleventh,
twelfth, thirteenth, fourteenth, fifteenth, or even
in the sixteenth century, a credit to Christianity ?
Was the condition of Christian lands, even in
the seventeenth century, anything to boast of ?

In every Christian history dealing with the
city at the time in question, it is stated that
the Caliph Omar, whose forces captured Alexandria in the year A.C. 640, ordered the priceless
manuscripts which on the accession to power
of the Christian Church were still safely stored
in its famous library, to be destroyed ; the Caliph
saying that if the works in question agreed with
the Koran they were superfluous, while if they
did not agree with it they were pernicious.   It
is the mistaken statement of a Christian Bishop.
The invaluable manuscripts in question, the sole
record of much of the knowledge of the history
and wisdom of the ancients, were destroyed in
the year A.C. 390 at the request of the Christian
Bishop of Alexandria, who, wishing to safe-
guard the position of the Church, had petitioned
the Emperor Theodosius for the requisite

authority. And this prelate's successor in the holy office was the Bishop whose clergy murdered Hypatia A.C. 415.

Then, and thus, were the Dark Ages inaugurated.

As to the libel on the great and magnanimous Omar, this was first given currency among Christians by Bishop Abulfaragius of Guba, in the thirteenth century ; and no such statement as his was made by any one of those who during the five hundred years immediately succeeding the capture of Alexandria by Omar, dealt with the history of that city. This silence upon their part is not to be wondered at, seeing that the priceless parchments in question were purposely destroyed by the Christians themselves just two centuries and a half before the army of Omar appeared upon the scene.

The libel in question, which is still given every currency in our schools, our histories, and our books of reference, is the more to be regretted inasmuch as Omar and his followers in the seventh century were more civilised than the Christians even of the eleventh century ; as can be seen by comparing the just behaviour of the Moslems, when they captured Jerusalem in the year A.C. 637, with the barbarities which the Crusaders inflicted upon Moslem and Jew alike when they captured the city in the year A.C. 1099. And during all the intervening centuries it was the Moslems, and not the Christians, who had held alight the torches of Science and Civilisation.

Moreover, though it is true that our present knowledge of the old Greek and Latin classics still extant is derived from manuscripts saved by Christian monks—saved, that is, from their own destroying hands—the revival of Science and of Learning in these latter days is due, not to the Christian Church, which to some extent stamped out Science and Learning, but to the Moslems against whom, in crusades begotten of ignorance and bigotry, all the so-called chivalry of Christendom was repeatedly flung in vain.

In vain; for it is not the Banner of the Cross but the Banner of the Crescent which for the last seven centuries has waved, and still waves, o'er Calvary. In vain; for not to the Three-in-One but to The Only, is dedicated the sacred building which crowns the topmost height of Mount Moriah.

Yet not altogether in vain. For the seven great Crusades, by helping to destroy the civilisation of the Saracens or Moors, and to develop marine intercourse between the nations, caused the evolution of a Christian civilisation, and now enables the Church to claim as its peculiar product a result achieved in spite of itself.

In spite of itself; for from the destruction of the Alexandrian Library in a.c. 390 and the murder of Hypatia, down to the persecutions of Galileo and of Bruno, and the invectives which, even as late as the present century, the Greek, Roman, and Protestant Churches have alike thundered forth against scientific facts and their promulgators, the Church has everywhere and always used its influence in as adverse a manner towards science as it dared.

But even if the reader has just possibly been able to free himself or herself sufficiently from the prejudices of a Christian education and environment to assimilate the foregoing facts, such an one may yet be quite unaware, or unable to realise, that Christianity as well as Civilisation existed before our era, and, like it, was not due either to the advent, life, or teaching, of Jesus the Nazarene.

This was admitted by more than one of the Fathers, however, and amongst others by the great St. Augustine. For toward the close of his remarkable career, that famous Bishop of Hippo wrote the following ever-to-be-remembered passage :—

"Again, in that I said 'This is in our time the Christian Religion, which to know and also follow is most sure and certain salvation'; it is affirmed in regard to this name, not in regard to the sacred thing itself to which the name belongs. For the sacred thing which is now called the Christian Religion existed in ancient times, nor indeed was it absent from the beginning of the human race until the Christ Himself came in the flesh, whence the true religion, which already existed, came to be called ' the Christian.' So when after His resurrection and ascension to heaven the Apostles began to preach and many believed, it is thus written, 'The followers were first called Christians at Antioch.' Therefore I said ' This is in our time the Christian Religion,' not because it did not exist in earlier times, but as having in later times received this particular name."[1]

---

[1] *Retractionum* S. Augustini, *Caput xiii., De Vera Religione.*

CHAPTER III.

" THE sacred thing which is now called the Christian Religion existed in ancient times, nor indeed was it absent from the beginning of the human race." Let us never forget this pregnant admission of one of the greatest of the Fathers, which by some happy chance has been allowed to come down to us.

For this confession of St. Augustine is an affirmation in plain and unmistakable terms by one who ought to have known, that what was in his time called the Christian Religion, existed long before the life, death, and alleged resurrection of Jesus, as preached by Paul in connection therewith, gave it the new name of Christian, and caused the followers of Paul at his head-quarters at Antioch to be called Christians; a name subsequently given to his followers else-where.

Nor was St. Augustine the only famous Father who is known to have admitted that what was called the Christian Religion was no new thing.

Even in the works of the great Ecclesiastical Historian, Eusebius, Bishop of Cæsarea, we come across a passage which states that—

"What is called the Christian Religion is neither new nor strange, but—*if it be lawful to testify as to the truth*—was known to the ancients."[1]

This, also, makes it plain that the Christian Religion was not the new thing it was supposed to be ; that the officials of the Christian Church kept this a secret from the rank and file ; and that what was and is known as Christianity existed ages before it was given that title, or was centred round the name and fame of Jesus the Nazarene by Paul of Tarsus and his followers.

In fact, judging from the admissions of St. Augustine, Eusebius, and other early Christian

---

[1] Eusebius, *Hist. Eccl.*, II. 5.

writers, what is called Christianity may under some name or other have existed as far back as the time when glorious Vega last shone as the Pole Star of the North, when Argo Navis had for so many centuries sailed southwards from the Sacred Sea that it had ceased to circle within sight of the dwellers even upon that sea's sunniest shores, when the Cross of the South could be seen even from Albion's Isle, when Columba the Dove no longer hovered upon the horizon of Egypt, and the land which was millenniums later to bear the burden of the pyramids had ceased for a time to be yearly gladdened by the vision of the peerless Dog Star heliacally rising as Herald of the Sun, and when even the glories of the Giant had so far forsaken Old Nile that the great Orion was at best but just visible from the site of Memphis as he led the Starry Host around the Heavenly Plains. Or perhaps, as St. Augustine intimates, the religion of the followers of Paul may have existed from the beginning; perchance even from that beginning when the Ancient Word first walked incarnate mid the trees of Earth and stood erect as Man.

"From the beginning," says St. Augustine. We, alas! know nothing of the Beginning. Christians have, it is true, annexed the alleged account of it by Moses which forms the commencement of the Scriptures held sacred by the Jews, but, as will be demonstrated further on, the Moses of the Bible appears to be a somewhat mythical personage, may be entirely a literary creation, and is not likely to have received as a revelation from the Infinite Spirit of the Universe, traditions which were current in Babylonia ages before the Israelitish tribe came into existence.

Now, not only do historical and scientific researches fail to bear out the statements to be found in that part of the so-called Book of Moses called Genesis, but even the Christian Church itself is obliged to make the fatal admission that part of same needs a new interpretation. For instance, a well-known Bishop writes as follows :—

"Darwin's conclusions startled pious minds at first as though they were subversive of the truth of revelation, but the panic has subsided, and it is recognised that the admission of Darwin's theories does not necessarily involve any contradiction of the inspired story of creation, though it may require a modification of the interpretation most commonly affixed to it." [1]

And it is evident (1) that the value of a revelation which is wrongly interpreted is small indeed ; (2) that if the Church has given a wrong interpretation of the first chapter of Genesis to the world for eighteen centuries, its authority upon other matters also is untrustworthy ; and (3) that as it is well known that the stories in the Bible of the Creation, the Fall, the Deluge, the Tower of Babel, and the Confusion of Tongues, were current among the Babylonians many centuries before Moses can have appeared upon the scene, the assumption that the Bible is an inspired revelation is—an assumption.

We know nothing of The Beginning. But we do know that Man lived upon this Earth many thousands of years before the date which the

---

[1] The Bishop Suffragan of Shrewsbury, *v. The Times*, *January* 31*st*, 1894.

Christian Church, upon the authority of its Scriptures, has assigned as that of the Creation.

According to the pronouncements of the Church during the last eighteen centuries, the genus Homo was not in existence six thousand years ago. But as a matter of fact, it is well known that at the very time Adam and Eve are by the Bible represented as being created, Mankind already existed, and in some lands were in a state of civilisation which it must have taken thousands upon thousands of years to have developed.

For it is the first step which costs. Given the civilisation of ancient Greece, Rome, Egypt, or Babylon, there was nothing wonderful in the civilisation of the eighteenth century of the Christian era. But given no such preceding civilisation, unnumbered ages must have elapsed ere the ascent of man could have been such as to have made possible the civilisation known to have existed in Accadia centuries before the alleged creation of Adam and Eve is fabled to have taken place.

When taking a survey of the traditions of the

dim and distant past, perhaps the two stories
most likely to arrest the attention of the average
inquirer would be those concerning Atlantis and
the Deluge.

Every well-informed person knows the story of
Atlantis as related by Plato, and has pondered
over his famous and circumstantial accounts of
the vast island which was swallowed up by the
relentless ocean. In one of those accounts Plato
says :—

"There was an Island situated in front of the
Straits which are by you called the Pillars of
Heracles, the Island was larger than Libya and Asia
put together, and was the way to the islands, and
from those you might pass to the whole of the
opposite continent which surrounded the true ocean,
for the sea which is within the Straits of Heracles is
only a harbour having a narrow entrance, but that
other is a real sea, and the surrounding land may
be most truly called a boundless continent. Now in
this Island of Atlantis there was a great and wonderful
empire . . . which had subjected the parts of
Libya within the columns of Heracles as far as
Egypt, and of Europe as far as Tyrrhenia. . . . But
afterwards there occurred violent earthquakes and

floods . . . and the Island of Atlantis . . . disappeared in the depths of the sea."[1]

This passage, with its description of the sea which extends from that part of Asia Minor then called Asia to the Pillars of Hercules, *i.e.*, the Mediterranean, as a mere gulf of the ocean outside those pillars, discloses a much better conception of the geography of the world than is usually credited to the ancients. But whether the story itself is a true one, or a baseless tradition, or a literary creation, there is no satisfactory evidence. It has, however, this one thing in its favour—that it might be true.

With regard to the story of the Deluge, however, we are upon a somewhat different footing. Whether the origin of all such traditions was or was not the Babylonian account of The Beginning from which the Jews borrowed the commencement of Genesis, traditions of a deluge vast enough to drown all the human race with some half dozen or so exceptions, have been found even among savage races. On the other hand, it is noteworthy

---

[1] Plato, *Timæus*: Jowett's translation.

that the ancient Egyptians, with all their knowledge of the past, and despite their acquaintance
with the version current among the Greeks,[1] and
no doubt with the older if not original one of the
Babylonians, had no such tradition. At any rate,
Manetho declared that his countrymen knew of
no such Deluge, and the testimony of the
thousands of inscriptions upon the ancient monuments to be found in the Land of the Nile has so
far borne him out.

As to the Deluge of the Bible narrative, which
is said to have covered the highest mountains,
such a story is plainly mythical. We know that
no great general collapse of the earth's surface
has taken place, and a deluge from any other
cause sufficient to cover the tops of the mountains
all over the earth would mean a sudden increase
of ten miles in the earth's diameter and an utter
disorganisation of the whole Solar system. Even
the sinking of an Atlantis would not cause the
submersion of Chimborazo, Everest, and Ararat;
and there is no evidence that even so minor a

---

[1] Pindar, *Ol.*, ix. 37; Ovid, *Met.*, I. 240; Lucian, *De Syrâ Deâ*;
Apollodorus, *Lib. I.*

catastrophe as that has occurred since the rise of Man.

Moreover, the idea that hundreds of reptiles, thousands of mammalia and birds, and hundreds of thousands of insects, in pairs, and representing the various orders and species, were saved in an Ark, is plainly absurd. And even those who do believe that this really happened, must surely at times join the rest of us in piously regretting that Noah did not use his influence to secure the barring-out of the elect representatives of certain species of reptiles and insects still extant.

It is, by the way, worthy of note that the originator of the story of the Deluge seems to have been unaware that many species of living creatures do not pair.

There are, too, multitudes of marine animals and littoral animals which an universal flood that covered the highest mountains would have utterly destroyed. As to the vegetable kingdom, also not provided for in the Ark, submergence under so great a weight of water would evidently have prevented the survival of many a plant still in existence.

It is, moreover, to say the least, difficult to see why an inspired revelation of the past should omit all reference to the last Glacial Epoch; which, unlike the alleged Deluge, we know has happened; and that, too, since the rise of Man.

As to the account of the alleged Deluge given in Genesis, there is one significant feature which is generally, if not always, overlooked. That feature is the great care taken to specify the exact days upon which Noah entered the Ark, left the Ark, and did or noticed this, that, or the other, while in the Ark.

Now even to the average Christian it must, if he or she ever thinks out such matters as these, appear curious that an inspired account of The Beginning should be so very careful to record the exact duration of the Deluge, and the time at which each of its incidents took place, and yet not so much as refer to the dates of the Confounding of Tongues and other remarkable events. To those, however, who can read between the lines, and to whom the history of the past is not a " fable agreed upon," but a science, there is here the outward and visible sign of an inward and hidden meaning.

The first worship was Nature worship. The first Gods were naturally the Sun, the Moon, the Stars, the Dawn, the Vault of Heaven, and other marvels or aspects of Nature. The first prophets were prophets of astronomical events. And probably the first " close corporation " in the shape of a priesthood was that of men whose leaders knew how to tell the face of the sky and compute the calendar; thus, in the eyes of the uninitiated, holding converse with the gods themselves.

Let us see if the account of the Deluge borrowed by the Jews from Babylon is not in reality an astronomical allegory; a story in which, as originally told, some of the astronomical knowledge of the remote ancestors of the Babylonians was set forth.

An analysis of the account in Genesis shows that the month spoken of in connection with Noah and his Ark was one of thirty days. For from the seventeenth of the second month to the seventeenth of the seventh month is stated to have been one hundred and fifty days.

The length of the month was never any secret, however, as any one could reckon from one new moon to another; though for the matter of that it was seldom allotted the number of days in a lunation. It was an arbitrary division of the year, varying in differing countries and in different ages; and as the year of most nations consisted of a number of days not exactly divisible by twelve, one month was usually made shorter than the other eleven, to prevent the twelfth month running on into the next year.

The length of the lunar year, so often adopted by the ancients, was also no secret; and for much the same reason. Any one could reckon it, and the calendar could not be fixed by it. The length of the solar year, so nearly as it can be expressed in days, was sometimes a secret and sometimes otherwise. The exact length of the solar year was usually a secret known only to a few chosen ones, and the exact length of the sidereal year was of course a greater secret still.

If, therefore, the Jewish version of the Babylonian legend of a Deluge is an old astronomical allegory, we might reasonably expect to find the year mentioned to be a lunar year, and the knowledge half hidden and half revealed the length of the solar year so far as it can be stated in days.

Now it is clear that in the twelfth and thirteenth verses of the eighth chapter of Genesis the same date is repeated, just as in verses three and four, and that the first day of the new year mentioned was the first day after the second period of seven days after the preceding forty days at the end of which Noah is said to have opened the window of the Ark. As that forty days is said to have commenced upon the first day of the *tenth* month, this would make the length of the year in question three hundred and twenty-four days ($30 \times 9 + 40 + 7 + 7$). But this is an absurd length, denoting the presence of an error in the Jewish version of the story.

Where, then, is the error? We might naturally expect to find it in the dropping of an unit, the common failing of the Jews when dealing with figures. And such it would appear to be.

As the period of one hundred and fifty days

is otherwise checked, and that of forty days is a well-known one, the only place where an unit could have been dropped is in verse five, where what is referred to as the tenth month was evidently not the tenth month. What then was the unit dropped here in recording the tens; or, to be quite accurate, the ten?

It could not have been more than one, for even two would mean a year of three hundred and eighty-four days; which is as absurdly out of it as one of three hundred and twenty-four. It must have been " one," and the month originally referred to not month ten but month eleven; which would mean a year of three hundred and fifty-four days —*i.e.*, a lunar year.

As for the hidden knowledge, this can now easily be seen. For as we are carefully told that Noah went into the Ark upon month two, day seventeen of one year, and came out upon month two, day twenty-seven of the next, reckoning the days both of entrance and of exit we have here a period of three hundred and sixty-five days, or a solar year.

The foregoing may appear to be a far-fetched

explanation of the peculiarity to which attention has been drawn, and no stress is laid upon it. Nevertheless it should not be considered by itself, but in connection with the more certain demonstrations to follow of the astronomical and allegorical character of various stories to be found in the Bible. And whatever its faults as an explanation of the very curious fact that in this particular story dates and times are so very carefully and frequently mentioned, while in the stories of the Creation, the Fall, the Confusion of Tongues, and elsewhere, nothing of the sort is referred to, it seems clear that it will hold the field. For it has no competitors.

As further evidence of the allegorical and astronomical character of the old Babylonian legend preserved for us by the Jews which has Noah for its hero, it should be pointed out that all the events mentioned in the legend of the Deluge are said to have taken place in either the six hundredth or the six hundred and first year of Noah's life ; that is, at the meeting point of two of those famous cycles of six hundred years so often referred to by ancient writers.

This cycle of six hundred years was often spoken of as the Great Year. Some nave sup- posed that the ancients thought it took that period to bring about a second time the same relative positions of the sun, moon, and earth. Others think it to have been arrived at as being 100 × 6 ; one hundred years being a *sæculum* or age, and six a key number with the Chaldæans, as shown by the six days at a time upon which they deemed it right to work, the sixty parts into which they divided the hour, and the 6 × 60 days of their year. Another theory is that it arose as a convenient and clear fraction of the Accadian or Chaldæan estimate of the length of the preces- sional period due to the oscillation of the earth's axis, which much longer cycle was also often spoken of as the Great Year.

It is not known for certain what the Chal- dæans—*i.e.*, the earlier Chaldæans—considered the length of the Precessional Year to be, but it is now computed at between twenty-five thousand and twenty-six thousand solar years ; in half of which time the seasons of course completely change in any given latitude. It must not be thought, however, that this regular effect of the precession of the equinoxes upon the seasons has been the cause of great glacial epochs or ice ages such as geologists tell us of, for such glacial epochs not only seem to have come at, from our limited point of view, irregular times, and to have been of different duration, but also to have extended over periods of time lengthy enough to have included several precessional years, and therefore all the minor changes alluded to.

That the precession of the equinoxes and the consequent change of the seasons were discovered thousands of years before our era is well known.

It is also noteworthy that the great walls of Babylon are said to have been built to keep out the Deluge which alternated with threatened destruction in the shape of fire every other six thousand years. This appears to have been founded upon a knowledge of the effects of the precession of the equinoxes.

We also learn that the Chaldæans spoke of a time when, once again—

" The land will be shrouded in the awful darkness of prolonged and stormy winter, and the saving rays

of the Sun-God will but feebly lighten the earth,
even at that once happy season of the year when in
the almost forgotten summers of the past the light
was greatest." [1]

As to the six hundred years' cycle to which
so much importance was attached in bygone ages,
and its connection with the story of Noah and
his Ark, it should be pointed out that the great
Jewish historian Josephus refers to it in the
following significant terms :—

" God afforded them (*i.e.*, the Patriarchs who lived
before the Deluge) a longer time of life on account
of their virtue, and the good use they made of it
in astronomical and geometrical discoveries, which
would not have afforded the time of foretelling unless
they had lived six hundred years ; for the Great Year
is accomplished in that interval." [2]

It will be seen that this reference of Josephus
to the cycle of six *sæcula* or ages, forming a Great
Year of six hundred ordinary years, directly
supports the contention herein set forth as to the
importance attached to that cycle in days of old,

---

[1] Berosus.   [2] Josephus, *Antiq. Jud.*, I., 3, 9.

and as to the significance of the fact that the waters are said to have been first dried up after the Deluge "in the six hundredth and first year, the first month, the first day of the month "; *i.e.*, the very moment a new Great Year began.

With a view to enabling the reader to see the allegorical and astronomical character of yet other Bible stories, it will be well to point out here that while the astronomer-priests of some nations which flourished in days of yore seem to have computed the rate at which the equinoxes precess at one degree in a *sæculum* or age of one hundred years, more skilful ones elsewhere appear to have variously estimated it at one degree in seventy-one or seventy-two years, the favourite estimate being one in seventy-two years. And this estimate of one degree in seventy-two years was a correct one. The rate is now known to be one degree in between seventy-one and seventy-two years, and the period in question to be much nearer seventy-two than seventy-one years.

Reminding the reader that the Jews had an unfortunate habit of quoting round numbers and leaving out the units, an example we follow in speaking of the seventy-two translators chosen by the High Priest Eleazar as the LXX. and of their work as the Septuagint, it may now be remarked that as an apprehension of the fact and rate of precession is, as it were, the key to astronomy, great importance would naturally have been attached in ancient days to the number signifying the rate of precession, and the number seventy-two might therefore be expected to be frequently met with in the traditions which have come down to us.

It is therefore curious to note that according to some authorities the army sent against Troy at the end of the proceedings had had in all seventy-two commanders, and that there has for thousands of years existed a tradition among the Jews that the world was after the Deluge divided into that number of countries. The number of Israelites who are represented as going down into Egypt seems also to have been the mystic number in question. (Compare Exod. i. 1-5 and Deut. x. 22 with Gen. xxxviii. 2.) Moreover, the sojourning of the Israelites, which according to the writer of the Epistle to the Hebrews commenced at the call of Abraham, is said to have lasted four hundred and thirty years, or six times $71\frac{2}{3}$; and this period of four hundred and thirty was divisible into two equal parts of two hundred and fifteen years, or three times $71\frac{2}{3}$, the time from the call of Abraham to the migration into Egypt being of that duration. Again, tradition tells us that the number of angels Jacob saw ascending the heavens was seventy-two. The number of Elders chosen by Moses was also seventy-two, the seventy given in the Jewish text being evidently due to the dropping of the unit, as the Sanhedrin of later days consisted of seventy-one members and a president. Preferring, for obvious reasons, the incorrect number of the Elders of Israel, the proper number of the Cardinals of him upon whose chair of St. Peter the soldiers of Napoleon are said to have found the signs of the Zodiac, who wears a triple crown as a sign that his rule extends even unto the skies, whose emblem as the vice-gerent of the Sun-God who crosses the Heavenly Equator twice a year—opening the Bottomless Pit of the South, Winter, or Hades at the Autumnal Equinox, and

Heaven at the Vernal Equinox, when he re-enters the North and ushers in the Summer—consists of two keys, and who, seated in the centre of the high altar, which in his cathedral church is at the West end of the building, looks out through the great Eastern entrance at the place of the Sun's rising, is said by the authorities at Rome to be seventy.

It is also noteworthy that the astronomer-priests of old mapped out the heavens into seventy-two divisions, that the Jewish High Priest sent seventy-two interpreters with the Book of the Law to Alexandria, and that those interpreters are said to have taken just seventy-two days in translating same into Greek ; that the Solumi of Darius were seventy-two in number, that the number of so-called apocryphal Hebrew Scriptures was seventy-two, that the sacred candlestick of the Jews had seventy—*i.e.*, seventy-two—ornaments, that the number of the heifers sacrificed at the Feast of Tabernacles was the same, and also the number of Rulers before Adam mentioned in the traditions of the Persians.

The number of Pliny's constellations was

seventy-two, the great standard work of the Babylonians upon astronomy, known to fame as *Observations of Bel*, was in seventy-two books, and the conspirators who were mystically said to have killed the still living Sun-God Osiris also numbered seventy-two.

And, most significant of all, it is well known to scholars that Jesus, as the alleged incarnation of the Sun-God, was said to have had seventy-two disciples; the original manuscripts giving that, and not seventy, as the number of those who were specially appointed in addition to the twelve. For instance, both the *Codex Vaticanus* and the *Codex Bezæ* give seventy-two, and not seventy, both in Luke x. i. and x. 17.

The twelve disciples of course represented the twelve constellations of the Zodiac or mansions of the Sun, and the corresponding twelve months of the year.

As to the other seventy-two disciples, of whose special mission to the cities of Israel we are given a long account in the tenth chapter of the Gospel "according to" St. Luke, it is noteworthy that we never hear of them again, although they are said to have been able to cast out demons and their names to have been written in heaven. The fact is their names *were* " written in heaven," and they were altogether heavenly, inasmuch as it is a Sun-God allegory, and they represented the years it takes for the place of the Sun-God at the Vernal Equinox to precess one degree of the Zodiac.

Nor, as already pointed out, is there anything to be wondered at in the fact that the rate of precession was in so many things allegorically shadowed forth ; for it was in days of old a great secret known only to the initiated, and both was, is, and will be, the master-key to the heavens and to heavenly knowledge.

The mysterious story of Enoch who " walked with God " and who " was not, for God took him," deserves a passing remark, as the fact that he is said not to have died but to have been taken is evidently meant to draw attention to a hidden meaning. This we find in the number of years he is said to have lived ere he was "taken" ; this being put at three hundred and sixty-five, the number of days in a solar year.

The year of the Accadians or ancient Babylonians was one of three hundred and sixty days ;
a supplemental month being added every six
years in order that the Calendar might be kept
something like accurate.

The month which was every six years doubled
in length was the one which corresponded to the
constellation of the Fish in the Zodiac. This is
why there are always two representations of the
symbol of this particular " mansion of the Sun."

Not a few scholars have held that the catastrophe required to cause the alleged universal
Deluge, also, by upsetting the relative position
and motion of the earth, caused the solar year to
be altered from exactly three hundred and sixty
days in length to the three hundred and sixty-five
days and a fraction it is now; the Accadian
Calendar, with its three hundred and sixty days,
and the Zodiac, with its three hundred and sixty
degrees, being relics of a pre-existing civilisation.
The occurrence since the rise of Man of a catastrophe great enough to have produced so astonish-
ing an effect, is, however, unproven. The theory
is obviously an absurd one.

And, whether the true one or not, a more natural and quite possible explanation of the supposed mystery as to why the Zodiac was divided into three hundred and sixty degrees, and the year into three hundred and sixty days to correspond with same, stares us in the face.

For the ancients worshipped both the Sun and the Moon, as the two great lights of heaven ; and three hundred and sixty days is the mean between the solar and lunar years. Taking the present values of the solar and lunar years—solar, from Vernal Equinox to Vernal Equinox, 365*d*. 5*h*. 48*m*. 45·51s. ; and lunar, from New Moon to New Moon twelve times, 354*d*. 8*h*. 48*m*. 32·20s.—and averaging them, shows the mean to be 359*d*. 19*h*. 18*m*. 38·85s. And that result is nearer to three hundred and sixty days than the solar year is to three hundred and sixty-five days or the lunar year to three hundred and fifty-four days.

Yet another key to the real nature of Genesis and other parts of the Bible is to be found in the famous dream of Joseph about twelve stars, " Behold the sun and the moon and the eleven stars made obeisance to me " (Gen. xxxvii. 9).

The eleven stars or constellations represented, we are told, the eleven brothers of Joseph. He, then, was the twelfth ; and the twelve stars or constellations referred to are those of the Zodiac.

All this is, to those initiated into such matters, yet more clearly shadowed forth in the words with which the dying Jacob or Israel is said to have blessed his twelve sons.

In this blessing Joseph is described as the one whose " bow abode in strength." That is, the constellation Sagittarius the Archer, who is represented as a bowman upon a horse, with his bow bent and the arrow ready to fly—*i.e.*, the bow abiding in strength.

In the Zodiac the next constellation to Sagittarius, the archer seated upon a horse, is Scorpio, the Scorpion or Serpent. In the Bible story we have Dan " a serpent by the way, an adder in the path, that biteth the horse heels, so that his rider shall fall backward." This is a clear reference to the Zodiac, which represents Scorpio in a position to attack the heel of the horse upon which Sagittarius rides.

As two of the twelve sons had to be coupled

together in order to represent the twins, this
would necessitate one being mentioned twice and
representing two constellations. Dan is accordingly mentioned twice. And as the next constellation to that of Scorpio the Serpent is Libra
the Balance, the second description applied to this
son is of course that of a judge : " Dan shall
judge his people as one of the tribes of Israel."

The next Zodiacal constellation to Libra is that
of Virgo, who is usually represented as holding
a full ear of corn. Accordingly the Bible gives
us Asher—*i.e.*, Asherah, the stellar goddess worshipped in different countries under the different
names Asherah, Ashtoreth, Astarte, Ishtar, Hera,
Aphrodite, and Venus—and says that Asher's
" bread shall be fat."

The next constellation to Virgo is Leo. The
dying patriarch is therefore said to have called
Judah a lion's whelp ; and the Lion of Judah
has passed into a proverbial expression.

Next to Leo the Lion, is Cancer the Crab,
represented in the Bible story by Zebulon, who
was to dwell " at the haven of the sea."

Gemini the Twins is the next constellation in

the Zodiac ; and to represent the same Simeon and Levi are coupled together : "Simeon and Levi are brethren."

Next to Gemini comes Taurus the Bull, to represent which the Bible story gives us Issachar "the strong ass couching down between two burdens," who " bowed his shoulder to bear " the yoke, these being references to the Oriental use made of the ox for ploughing and other purposes.

Aries the Ram is the next constellation. The same is represented by Naphtali, which name is a play upon *taleh*, the Hebrew word for Ram.

We next come to Pisces the Fish, to represent whom we are given Gad. Now Gad is simply Dag reversed in order to keep some semblance of mystery in the allegorical story, and Dag means—the Fish.

Aquarius the Waterer comes next in the Zodiac, where he is represented as a man with an urn pouring out water. Accordingly we find Reuben likened to water, or rather, as the original signifies, to the pouring out of water.

Next and last is Capricorn, represented by Benjamin. As in the Egyptian Zodiac Capricorn was figured as a goat with a wolf's head, Benjamin is naturally described as a ravening wolf.

Another noteworthy point is that not only did the Israelites of old consider the bull, heifer, or calf to be the correct form in which to image forth the God they worshipped, but according to tradition the symbols of four tribes were placed one each at the four corners of the Israelitish camp, and the four selected tribes were those whose symbols were respectively the Bull, the Waterpourer, the Serpent, and the Lion. For the symbols in question are those of the constellations at the cardinal points of the Zodiac when the Sun is in Taurus.

The care with which the number twelve was kept to the front by the astronomer-priests who taught this allegory of the twelve sons of Israel to the people they ruled over and called children of Israel, is also significant of much. Not liking to couple Simeon and Levi together as the progenitors of but one tribe between them, they accordingly got over the difficulty by ingeniously omitting Joseph and attributing a separate tribe to each of Joseph's two sons, Ephraim and

Manasseh. They had the people divided into thirteen tribes, and called the thirteen " twelve."

Even the Fathers seem to have been to some extent aware of the allegorical and astronomical nature of the Bible account of the early history of the world in general and the so-called Children of Israel in particular. For instance, we find St. Clement of Alexandria writing about the ornaments worn by the Israelitish High Priest, admitting that—

" The bright emeralds upon the ephod signify the Sun and Moon ; and the twelve precious stones arranged in four rows describe to us the Zodiacal circle relatively to the four seasons of the year." [1]

Yet further evidence of the allegorical character of the alleged twelve sons of Israel, and of the mythical nature of the whole story, can be found in the works of Josephus. For in one passage in particular the great Jewish historian, referring to the breastplate of the High Priest, lets drop a hint of great significance and importance. He says :—

---

[1] Clem. Alex., *Strom.* v.

" Whether any one wish to refer the twelve stones to the twelve months, or to the same number of constellations in the circle which the Greeks call the Zodiac, he will not wander far from the real meaning," [1]

Having dealt with the seventy-two descendants and twelve sons of Israel—whose name signifies "prevailing over El" the Sun-God, and who seems to be an allegorical representation either of the Zodiac or of Cronos—*i.e.*, Old Father Time—who are said to have gone down into Egypt, let us now turn our attention to the story of Moses and the Exodus.

That the Israelites were descendants of slaves who escaped from Egypt, that those slaves had a leader to head them in their revolt and subsequent march, and that such leader was a man called Moses, would not in itself be an evidently improbable story.

But the Bible account is that the escaping people had with them 603,550 able-bodied male adults over twenty years of age, and available for

---

[1] Josephus, *Antiq. Jud.*, III.

fighting purposes, without counting the men of the tribe of Levi (Numb. i. 45-47). Adding all the males under twenty, the Levites, the infirm old men, the men otherwise incapacitated for taking the field against their enemies, and all the females, we find that the total number of the Israelites referred to in the Bible could not have been less than three millions. Such a story is plainly mythical.

For instance, the exodus of so many people from the land of Egypt would have depopulated it. And the march of so many men, women, and children, across either barren or hostile countries, or across fertile or friendly countries, would even in these times be impossible.

The alleged exodus of the Israelites is also shown to be mythical by what we know of the past history of the lands of Egypt and of Canaan.

According to the dates kindly supplied in many copies of the English Bible, and founded upon the calculations of Archbishop Usher, the exodus of the Israelites took place in the year 1491 B.C. And the *Encyclopædia Britannica* says :—

" According to the Old Testament the Exodus took place 480 years before the building of Solomon's Temple, and 960 years before the end of the Babylonian captivity." [1]

This would mean 960 + 536, or about 1496 B.C.

Many Christians, however, finding anything like the Bible date an awkward one to reconcile with other statements in the Bible, declare that the Exodus must have taken place as far back as the middle of the seventeenth century B.C.; Smith's *Dictionary of the Bible* declaring in favour of the year B.C. 1652.

Now it is admitted that Eli was appointed Judge about the middle of the twelfth century B.C. It is also generally admitted that the famous Deliverance by Samuel occurred about the year 1104 B.C., the accession of Saul about the year 1094 B.C., the death of Samuel about the year 1061 B.C., the accession of David about the year 1054 B.C., the capture of Jerusalem or Mount Zion by King David about the year 1045 B.C.—we are asked to believe that the Israelites

---

[1] *Encyc. Brit.,* " *Israel.*

captured the land of Canaan four hundred years or more before they captured Mount Zion—and the founding of the Temple about the year 1004 B.C.

Now the Tel-el-Amarna tablets, which date back to the fifteenth century B.C., conclusively prove that Canaan was then an Egyptian province ; these tablets being despatches from the rulers of Jerusalem and other cities, to their suzerain Amenophis IV., Pharaoh of Egypt. The alleged Exodus had therefore not taken place then.

Later on we come to the time of Rameses II., who reigned about the middle of the fourteenth century B.C., and is usually called the Pharaoh of the Oppression. From a monument in the neighbourhood of Saijdeh, near the Sea of Tiberias and on the road to Damascus, which has long been reverenced as the Stone of Job, we learn that the rule of the Pharaoh in question, Rameses II., Ra-user-ma-setep-en-Ra, the beloved of the Sun-God, extended a hundred miles or more beyond Jerusalem.

In yet later times we find Rameses III. recording that about the year 1270 B.C.—only a hundred years before the judgeship of Eli-- several nations invaded Canaan and marched upon him, he defeating them upon the borders of Egypt, and pursuing them as far north as Aleppo and Carchemish. He mentions no such people as the Israelites, and, what is still more notable, the Bible does not record this march of allied nations through Canaan, and their subsequent pursuit through the same territory by Rameses III.

As this last event occurred centuries after the alleged Exodus under Moses and capture of Canaan by his successor Joshua, and so short a time before the judgeship of Eli, the only rational conclusion is that the said Exodus and capture of Canaan are mythical stories.

In fact, the Israelites and Canaanites appear to have been one and the same, "Children of Israel" being the name given by their astronomer-priests to certain Canaanitish tribes who combined against a common enemy in the days of Eli and Samuel, and who did not gain a complete ascendency over the others till King David captured Mount Zion from the Jebusites.

Seeing, therefore, that the commencement of the Bible is plainly mythical, let us still further study the astronomical lore of the ancients. Let us see whether much of the religion, as well as of the history, of the Bible, be not astronomical allegory.

As has been pointed out before, a knowledge of astronomy was at first naturally confined to a very few. And as it included the power to forecast events in the heavens, where the Gods were supposed to reside, it gradually elevated a select few into the position of mediators between the Gods and Mankind. These had disciples and assistants, and formed a close corporation, or, at any rate, a distinct class, only the innermost circle of which possessed any real knowledge of astronomy.

Thus, in every land, arose a Priesthood. And in every land these middlemen, mediators, readers of the heavens, interpreters of the Gods, prophets, or priests, were, thanks to the power of their leaders to forecast astronomical events, and to the utter ignorance of all save themselves, able in days of yore to impose their authority upon the people, and even to make puppets of the kings.

And just as a knowledge of astronomy was the origin of priests and the basis of their authority, in like manner was that same astronomical lore the real origin and basis of their revelations, whether concerning an unknown past or an unknown future.

Judaism and Christianity being based upon such revelations, it is clear that to arrive at their inner meaning a knowledge of ancient astronomical lore is necessary. And the more so inasmuch as the masses have ever been taught in allegories or parables, in order that " seeing, they may see and not perceive, and hearing, they may hear and not understand " (Mark iv. 11, 12).

Now the key to Christianity is to be found in the Zodiac.

The Zodiac, which appears to have been first so called by the Greeks, was said by Hipparchus and Ptolemy to have been of unknown origin and of " unsearchable antiquity." It is a map of, or referring to, the stars in that circular pathway around the heavens from which neither the Sun, nor the Moon, nor any of the Planets visible to the naked eye, was ever known to stray; these stars having from time immemorial been divided into twelve groups or constellations, forming certain fanciful figures of men and animals. Such figures naturally could not exactly fit in with each other, and differed largely in extent.

Hipparchus, desiring a more scientific division of the Zodiac, divided it into twelve "signs" of exactly thirty degrees each. These signs are, very unfortunately, named after the constellations, and much confusion results.

The confusion occasioned by calling twelve divisions of the Zodiac exactly similar in size to each other and touching their neighbours at all points of an imaginary dividing line, by the names for thousands of years previously given to twelve unequal divisions of the Zodiac of various shapes and in one sense not touching their neighbours at all—as can be seen by referring to any ancient Zodiac upon which the various figures are drawn—has been increased tenfold by the fact that, as at the time of Hipparchus the place of the Vernal Equinox happened to be amongst the stars forming the constellation Aries, he arranged his new Zodiac or map of the Sun's pathway so that the Equinoctial point in question should be at the first degree of his division or sign called Aries, whereupon astronomers, following his lead, have ever since fabled that the Equinoctial Point was and is the " First of Aries," although the place of the Vernal Equinox, being affected by the movement called the Precession of the Equinoxes, moves from year to year between $\frac{1}{25000}$th and $\frac{1}{26000}$th part of the great circle, and is now in the constellation Pisces.

The twelve constellations of the Zodiac were called Mansions of the Sun, and the Sun-God was supposed to inhabit each Mansion in turn during his annual journey round the heavens. In one, as, after the winter solstice, the first sign of the Sun's return from the South could be perceived, he was fabled as " born "; in another, at the Vernal Equinox, at the Sun's Passover or cross-over from South to North, he was represented as transfixed upon the Equator; in yet another, as taking his seat at the right hand of the All-Father, and showering down upon mankind the harvest blessings due to the warmth of summer.

The origin of the twelvefold division both of the Zodiac and of the Year was of course the fact that in each solar year there are twelve "moons." As each succeeding new or full moon takes place about a twelfth part of the Zodiac from where the preceding one did, it was obviously the natural arrangement, when dividing the Zodiac, to divide same into twelve. Hence the twelve constellations of the Zodiac, and the corresponding twelve months of the Year.

But when was the Year to commence, and which was to be the "beginning of months"?

Here again, to account for the decisions of the ancients—some of whom reckoned time by lunar years of three hundred and fifty-four days, some by solar years of three hundred and sixty-five days, and some by solar-lunar years of three hundred and sixty days, the Calendar being kept in something like accord with the seasons by various intercalations—we have but to con-

sider what was the most natural decision for
those Nature worshippers to arrive at.

For the ancients, as for us, every year was
first and foremost separated into the two great
divisions of summer and winter. And as their
ability to make long journeys in a short time,
and their means of protection against climatic
changes, were but small compared with ours,
the ancients naturally welcomed the one, and
hated the other, with feelings far deeper than
ours.

Now summer and winter in this Northern
Hemisphere of the earth, in which all the great
civilisations known to us have flourished, are due
to the fact that for about half the year the Sun
is in the corresponding Northern Hemisphere of
the heavens, the Sun being longer above the
horizon in consequence, and its rays, coming
more nearly at right angles to our atmosphere,
having less of same to penetrate, and more
effect upon the earth, with the result that summer
is produced ; while in the other half of the year,
the Sun being in the Southern Hemisphere of
the heavens, its rays in our northern latitudes

are less powerful, and winter is the consequence.

There are two great phenomena connected with summer and winter, either of which might naturally have been selected as the commencement of the year by the ancients.

The first of these is the " birth " of the Sun at the solstice in mid-winter, when the Sun, having reached its southernmost destination, commences its return to the north, and is therefore, in the old Sun-God myths and allegories, spoken of as " born." This event at the commencement of our era took place on December 25th, before the dawn, but, owing to the effects of the precession of the Equinoxes, now takes place three or four days earlier.

The Sun-God was represented as being in the hands of the Powers of Darkness for six months of the year—viz., from the Autumnal Equinox, when the Sun first begins to sink into the south, until the Vernal Equinox, when the Sun rises again out of it.

It was as the time of the Vernal Equinox drew near and the Sun approached the Equator, that the great struggle between the Powers of Darkness and the Sun-God, who was naturally hailed as the Saviour, was represented as taking place. From the moment the Sun's disc touched the Equator upon the south side, until it got clear of it upon the north side, the Sun-God was represented as transfixed upon the Equator, or by the Equator, and the Powers of Darkness as apparently getting the better of the conflict. Only apparently, however, for though some, borrowing the idea from the winter solstice, when at the death of the old year the Sun is stationary for a considerable time, and was spoken of as dead, fabled that as the result of the conflict the Sun-God was three days in the tomb, yet all agreed that soon after the transfixion the Sun-God triumphantly rose again, and that it was by his crossing he conquered.

In Judaism the conflict and its result were spoken of as the Passover or Cross-over; in Christianity the two things are distinguished from each other, the conflict being called the Crucifixion and the result being called the Resurrection.

As summer and its harvest, or, in other words,

the salvation of Mankind, depended upon the Sun-
God passing over the Equator, that is, surviving
his transfixion on or by the Equator and rising
again in the north above us, the victory of the
Saviour of the World was naturally deemed the
more important of the two phenomena mentioned,
and was that most generally fixed upon as decid-
ing when the year should be said to commence.
Hence the month of the Vernal Equinox, when the
Jews held their feast of the Passover or Cross-
over, was the one they called " the beginning of
months."

Now the position of the Sun at the Vernal
Equinox alters slightly from year to year owing
to the effects of precession. Since about the
commencement of our era it has been slowly
passing through the constellation Pisces the Fish ;
previous to that it was for thousands of years in
the constellation Aries the Ram, or male Lamb,
of God ; and before that it was for thousands of
years in Taurus the Bull. The exact dates it is
impossible to give, because the divisions of the
constellations are ill defined.

The average duration of each of such ages as

those in question is of course the precessional
year divided by twelve, or between two thousand
one hundred and two thousand two hundred
years. The duration of any given age can, for
the reason mentioned, only be very roughly
estimated. It would be fairly safe, however, to
say that the age of Taurus commenced centuries
before the date assigned to Adam; certainly not
later.

The Zodiac was undoubtedly planned before
the Biblical date of the Biblical Creation. It is
based upon the assumption that the place of the
Vernal Equinox is where the Sun enters the
constellation Taurus. Taurus the Bull is, therefore, its leading constellation.

It was this fact that, for thousands of years,
and at the time the Zodiac was first planned out,
the place of the Vernal Equinox, of the victory
of the Sun-God, of the Cross of the Saviour
of the World, was in Taurus, which in ancient
times caused the Bull to be almost universally
venerated as the symbol of the Sun-God and of
Deity.

After some two or three thousand years the

place of the Vernal Equinox had visibly passed from Taurus to Aries, and we accordingly find the astronomer-priests introducing the Ram or male Lamb as a sacred animal, and one to be utilised for purposes of sacrifice. But the Bull remained the symbolic representation of the Sun-God or Saviour of the World, not only throughout the age of Taurus, but almost if not quite to the end of the age of Aries also. And though Paul and his followers, in the Gospels they attributed to Matthew, Mark, Luke, and John, and in other writings, represent John the Baptist and others as speaking of the alleged incarnation of the Sun-God as the Lamb of God, and themselves so speak of him ; and yet later followers of Paul, realising that even the age of Aries the Ram or male Lamb of God had passed away, and the place of the conflict between the Sun-God and the Powers of Darkness moved into Pisces, spoke of the Christ as the Fish, and regarded the Fish as His symbol ; yet the main ideas arising from the original planning of the Zodiac, and for thousands of years preached by the astronomer-priests of every land, could never be disestablished,

and to this day form an important part of the
faiths of Mankind.

It ought here to be pointed out that the Cross
was not regarded as the symbol of the Christ
until Constantine made it so in the fourth century,
and is not included in Clement of Alexandria's
list of Christian symbols. Until the time of
Constantine, the Fish (or *two fishes*) was universally regarded as the symbol of the Christ, but it
was then gradually dropped in favour of the now
generally accepted Cross.

The fact that the Christ was in the first three
centuries usually represented as a Fish is of
itself significant ; and the fact that among the
Christian symbols of that date two fishes occur
almost as frequently as one, seems even more
clearly to demonstrate that the Sun-God in Pisces
is referred to.

It should also be noted that Jesus is never
represented as eating any other kind of animal
food than fish; that Christians, for reasons unknown to themselves, regard fish as holy food,
and the only kind of animal food permissible upon
fast days ; that not only did Tertullian call the

Christ "our great Fish," Origen declare that the
Christ was "allegorically called the Fish," and
St. Augustine, Jerome, and other Fathers, speak
of Him as the Fish, but that it was often as being
Fish that they spoke of Him as divine food ; that
upon ancient Christian tombs are found, under
representations of the symbolical two fishes, such
inscriptions as " The Fish of the living"; and
that in the famous inscription discovered in the
ancient Christian cemetery at Autun, the Christ
is called "the heavenly Fish," "the Saviour of
the saints," "the honey-sweet food," the "Lord
and Saviour," and the " Light of them for whom
the hour of death is past " ; the word Fish occur-
ring as the name of the Christ four times in the
text, and once—acrostically—in the initial letters.

Returning from this digression, it may be
pointed out that the idea that the Bull led the
way is enshrined even in the glorious verse of
Virgil. For it will be remembered that he
wrote :—

"Candidus auratis aperit cum cornibus annum
Taurus—— "

As to the ideas first preached in the age of

Taurus, at the commencement of which—*i.e.*,
before the Bible date of the creation of Adam—
the Zodiac is known to have been planned out,
these are perhaps best considered from the point
of view of the Accadian Calendar.

But let us first note the following admissions
of a distinguished prelate of the Church, regarding
the antiquity of the Accadian Civilisation. In a
Visitation Charge to his clergy, the Lord Bishop
of Manchester made the following memorable
remarks :—

" Now if these dates are accepted, to what age of
the world shall we assign the formation of that
Accadian civilisation and literature which so long
preceded Sargon I. and the statutes of Sirgullah ? I
can best answer you in the words of the great
Assyriologist, F. Hommel. ' If,' he says, ' the Semites
were already settled in Northern Babylonia (Accad)
in the beginning of the fourth thousand B.C. in
possession of the fully developed Shumiro—Accadian
culture adopted by them—a culture, moreover, which
appears to have sprouted like a cutting from Shumir
—then the latter must be far, far older still, and have
existed in its *completed* form in the fifth thousand B.C.,
an age to which I unhesitatingly ascribe the South

Babylonian incantations.' . . . Who does not see
that such facts as these compel us to remodel our
whole idea of the past ? " [1]

The Bishop of Manchester had previously
pointed out to his clergy, that in the days of
Sargon I. and Naram Sin, who lived in the age
the Bible allots to Adam, the language of Accad
had already ceased to be the tongue of the people,
and was a learned dialect like the Latin of the
Middle Ages. And it will be seen from that
portion of his charge which has been quoted,
that he admits the existence in the Babylonia of
the days of Adam of a civilisation which is known
to have existed long before the alleged date of
Adam's creation, and must have taken many
thousands of years to have developed.

Harking back to the subject of the Zodiac, we
find that in the Accadian Calendar Taurus was
called " the Directing Bull," showing that it was
considered the constellation of the month which
began the year. This is confirmed by the fact
that the constellation opposite to same, now

[1] Visitation Charge delivered at Blackburn, July 1889, by the
Lord Bishop of Manchester.

known as the Scorpion or Serpent, was called the star—*i.e.*, the constellation—"opposite to the foundation."

And the key to Christianity lies in this fact, that in the Zodiac or Map of Heaven the Scorpion or Serpent was the Opposer of the Sun-God, the usherer in of Winter as the Sun-God was of Summer, the Prince of Darkness as the Sun-God was of Light, the would-be Destroyer as the Sun-God was the would-be Saviour.

A curious illustration of the persistence of once widely accepted ideas ages after their origin and meaning have been forgotten, lies in the fact that Christians are invariably careful to represent their Devil, or Evil One, or Opponent of the Saviour, as having a barbed tail. Even when they represent him in the form of a man and put him in coat, vest, and trousers, the barbed tail can be seen, protruding somewhere or other, however hard the Prince of Darkness may be trying to hide it. Christians know not what they do when they represent their Prince of Darkness with, and recognise him by, a barbed tail. The barb is the sting of the Zodiacal Scorpion.

Remembering these things, and also that the Christianity of the last eighteen and a half centuries has been Pauline, that Paul's Epistles were written long before the Gospels, that the Gospels were doubtless written by his followers, and that all we know of Jesus, the Jew who said, "The Scribes and Pharisees sit in Moses' seat : all therefore whatsoever they bid you observe, that observe and do" (Matt. xxiii. 2, 3), and who was himself an observer of the Mosaic Law, and from first to last taught that it should be obeyed, comes to us through followers of a Jew who denounced the Law, let us consider for a moment what Paul taught.

If we turn to the first chapter of his Epistle to the Colossians we find him telling them to give thanks to the All-Father for making them meet to be partakers of the inheritance of the saints "in light," and for delivering them from the "power of darkness." And in verse 23 Paul exhorts them not to be moved away from the hope of the gospel—*i.e.*, from the hope of the glad tidings, "which was preached to every creature under heaven," in verse 26 declaring such

glad tidings to be a revelation of " the mystery
which hath been hid from ages and generations."

Now the glad tidings of the birth and resurrection of a poor Jewish Teacher called Jesus the
Nazarene, had not been preached to " every
creature which is under heaven "; nor, as it
should be translated, to " every creature in the
whole creation."

And while, upon the one hand, the gospel or
glad tidings preached by Jesus was most certainly
not that of His birth and resurrection, upon the
other hand none would more strongly than He
have denounced Paul and his followers for breaking the Ten Commandments and keeping holy
not the seventh day but the first.

Why did Paul break with the Jewish observance of the Sabbath or seventh day, and keep
the first ? Was it not because that day in the
Roman Calendar was Dies Soli, the Day of the
Sun ?

The fact is that Christians are followers not
of Jesus but of Paul; that the Gospels were
written after Paul by followers of Paul who
improved upon Paul, inventing stories of the

angel's notification that the first-born son of Mary
would be God incarnate, and to the effect that
Jesus was born of a virgin, that an angelic host
proclaimed His birth to shepherds, that a star
attracted wise men from a far-off land and
stopped over a given building pointing out where
Jesus lay, that God's voice was heard from heaven
proclaiming Jesus to be His Son, that Moses and
Elijah came down from heaven and conversed
with Jesus upon a mountain, that Jesus was
transfigured or metamorphosed and shone as the
Sun, that Jesus did this, that, and the other famous
miracle, and that He finally ascended to heaven
in bodily form, of all which wonders Paul was
clearly ignorant ; that while Jesus taught obedi-
ence to the Law of Moses, Paul was an apostate
Jew ; that what Paul taught was but a new
version of the old, old story of the conflict
between light and darkness, and of the Sun-God's
triumph ; that, influenced by the teachings of the
great Jewish philosopher Philo, he tried to
reconcile the religion of his race with the philosophy of the Greeks ; that he adopted as his own
the noble conception of a non-national religion

which should embrace all Humanity as beings
" made of one blood " ; that he hit upon the
ingenious idea of uniting in one the various
conceptions of the Sun-God worshipped by the
illiterate masses of every land, the Logos or Word
of God speculated upon by the philosophers, and
the Christ or Anointed One which members of
His own race hoped would arise to throw off the
Roman yoke and restore the kingdom of David ;
that he accordingly made out that the Sun-God,
the Logos, and the Christ, had been incarnated in
the person of a famous Jewish teacher just passed
away ; that the real Jesus was little more than
the frame upon which Paul and his followers
hung their theatrical effects ; and that their
Kurios or Lord, the well-known appellation of
the Sun-God, was their particular conception of
the Sun-God.

CHAPTER IV.

THE HEBREW SCRIPTURES.

IN the original text of the Old Testament writings there are no less than seven different frequently recurring words which, in the translations given to Mankind, are, despite their difference, rendered as if all meaning " Lord " or " God."

Those words are El, Eloah, Elah, Elohim, Adonai, Jah, and Jehovah.

The words El, Eloah, Elah, Jah, and Jehovah, are in the singular form ; and Elohim and Adonai in the plural.

El, a well-known appellation of the Sun-God in days of old, is translated as " God " in our Bibles, as are both Eloah and Elah. Elohim, the plural of the foregoing, is also translated as " God." Adonai is in many cases translated as " Lord,"

but in one instance is translated as "God." Jah
is once translated as "Jah," and, although essentially a name rather than a title, forty-three times
as "Lord." Jehovah, also a proper noun, is
translated a few times as "Jehovah," a great
many times as "Lord," and in many other places
as "God."

Concerning El, it may be remarked that Eusebius
tells us that the Canaanites called their chief God
Elion,[1] and that Damascius wrote to the effect
that—

"The Phœnicians and Syrians name Cronus 'El'
and 'Bel;'"[2]

while we all know that the Greek word for Sun
was Elios, there being no letter in the original for
the aspirate *H* usually added.

As a matter of fact, El, like On, was an appellation of the Sun-God. Or, to adhere to the
Zodiacal cult, El was an appellation of the
Sun-God, and On an appellation of his opponent
the Prince of Darkness. Hence El was an affix

---

[1] *Præp. Evan.*, I. 10, 36.   [2] *Apud Photium.*

or prefix of good omen, and frequently used, while On was one of bad omen, and more or less reserved for Abaddon himself.

The connection of El and On is undoubted, and it is quite clear that On was worshipped as well as El. As even On was the Sun, this is not surprising. And accordingly we find Joseph, though a devout worshipper of El, represented in the Bible as marrying the daughter of a priest of On, and Moses as making a Serpent of Brass an image of deity, which is said to have been worshipped by the Israelites right down to the days of Hezekiah, and even then to have been destroyed, not as an incorrect representation, but because it was only a representation.

The relationship between El and On is also shown by the fact that On, the Egyptian City of the Sun, was called Eliopolis (pronounced *Heliopolis*) by the Greeks. Moreover, two names seem to have been given to the spot where Israel is said to have had his famous dream, and one of them to have been Bethaven or Beth-av-On, as opposed to Beth-El (Josh. xviii. 12 ; Hosea iv. 15, v. 8, x. 5) ; while the present name is Beitin ; an evolution, one would think, rather of Beth-On than of Beth-El. And we are told that in days of yore the spot was called Eli-Oun.[1]

As to Adonai, the kinship of this word to Adonis is well known. And Adonis also signified "the Lord." Moreover, Adonis was a Sun-God as well as El, Eloah, Elah, or Elohim.

We now come to the names Jah and Jehovah. And it may be as well to point out at once that the proper pronunciation and spelling of Jah is Ia, pronounced *yah*, as in Alleluia ; and of Jehovah, Iaou, pronounced *yah-hoo*.

Owing to the great similarity of the two Hebrew letters *cheyth* and *he*, it is a matter of dispute whether the English equivalents of the four letters of the sacred tetragrammon are IHVH or IEVE, and those of the letters of its supposed diminutive IH or IE. But that the sacred name IEVE was pronounced more like *yah-hoo* than Jehovah, and IE more like *yah* than Jah, can easily be shown.

For instance, the famous and learned Clement

[1] Sachoniatho.

of Alexandria, who flourished at the end of the second century of the Christian era, refers to the tetragrammon or four-lettered name of the Hebrew deity, as—

"'That four-lettered mystic name, called Iaou, which is interpreted, He who is and will be." [1]

Irenæus, who lived at if anything a yet earlier epoch, tells us that Iao was the form used by the Gnostics to signify the God of the Hebrews.[2]

Epiphanius, who lived in the fourth century, renders ιενε and ιε as Iabe and Ia. He says—

" He who was, and is, and always is, as He (Iabe or Ia) interprets it to Moses, Thou shalt say to them, He who is, sent me." [3]

Theodoret, who wrote in the fifth century, says that—

" It is written by four letters, and is therefore called tetragrammon. The Samaritans pronounce it Iabe, but the Jews pronounce it Ia." [4]

---

[1] *Strom.*, v. 666.
[2] *Adv. Hær.*
[3] *Adv. Hær.*, 20.
[4] *Com. Exodus.*

And elsewhere he writes concerning—

" Ia, the Lord, or He who is." [1]

Philo, the great Jewish philosopher who lived before, and during, the lifetime of Jesus, and whose attempts to reconcile Greek philosophy and Judaism, by exciting the enthusiasm of Paul, seem to have been the real source of the inspiration of the founder of Christianity, tells us that the sacred name was pronounced like the Greek Ieuo.[2]

In ancient Babylonian contract tables the name is given as Ia ; Bel-Yaii, Bel is Ia. And both the Moabite Stone and the Assyrian monuments bear witness that the name of the deity of the Hebrews—and others—was pronounced Yahoo.

As the sacred name in question was a four-lettered one, perhaps the best rendering of IEVE would be Iaou. Instead, therefore, of speaking of Jehovah or Jah, let us in future use the words Iaou and Ia.

Now an examination of the original text of the

---

[1] *Quæst.* 15 *in Ex.*   [2] *Sanch.* 2.

Hebrew Scriptures, as at present known to us, shows us that the seven names mentioned occur the following numbers of times in the Pentateuch—

The word El occurrs 16 times in Genesis, 7 times in Exodus, not once in Leviticus, 10 times in Numbers, and 13 times in Deuteronomy.

The word Eloah occurs twice in Deuteronomy.

The word Elah does not occur at all till later on in the Old Testament.

The plural form Elohim occurs 183 times in Genesis, 73 times in Exodus, 26 times in Leviticus, 18 times in Numbers, and 21 times in Deuteronomy.

The word Adonai occurs 6 times in Genesis, 5 times in Exodus, and once in Numbers, but not in Leviticus, nor in Deuteronomy.

The name Ia occurs twice in Exodus.

The name Iaou occurs 135 times in Genesis, 360 times in Exodus, 285 times in Leviticus, 390 times in Numbers, and 234 times in Deuteronomy.

The combination of Adonai-Elohim occurs twice in Genesis and twice in Deuteronomy.

The combination of Iaou-Elohim occurs 29 times in Genesis, 38 times in Exodus, 26 times in Leviticus, 6 times in Numbers, and 315 times in Deuteronomy.

This analysis reveals the significant fact that the name Iaou or Jehovah—a name which, as even Professor Ewald has admitted, "has no clear radical significance in Hebrew," [1]—although stated in the Bible to have been revealed to the Israelites at the time of the Exodus, occurs over a hundred and fifty times in Genesis.

As to the famous passage, " I appeared unto Abraham, unto Isaac, and unto Jacob, by the name (title) of God Almighty " (El Shaddai, the Sun-God and Thunderer) ; " but by My name Jehovah was I not known unto them " (Exod. vi. 3), to account for the frequent use of the name in question in Genesis by saying that Moses was inspired to write Genesis after the name had been revealed to him, is no explanation whatever of the discrepancy pointed out.

Moreover, Abraham and other ancestors of the

---

[1] *Gesch.*, d. vi. II. 203.

Israelites are in Genesis repeatedly stated to have called upon the God Iaou or Jehovah. And even as early as Gen. iv. 26 we read—

" *Then* began men to call upon the name of"— Iaou.

Nor is this all; for we are told that while the Israelites were still upon the way to Canaan, and while Moses was still alive, the King of Moab sent to a Midianitish diviner or soothsayer named Balaam; and that this very God Iaou came to Balaam in the night and conversed with him. Various other talks between Balaam and the God named Iaou or Jehovah are reported, and in Numb. xxiii. 4 the Bible states that Balaam went to meet Iaou, and that Iaou met him. He is also represented as using Iaou as the name of the Sun-God, saying " El brought them up out of Egypt. . . . All that Iaou speaketh that must I do " (Numb. xxiii. 22-26), and " How shall I curse whom El hath not cursed, or how shall I defy whom Iaou hath not defied ? " (Numb. xxiii. 8.)

And in Numb. xxii. 18 this Midianitish priest

of the Sun-God is represented as saying, "I cannot go beyond the word of Iaou *my* God."

The theory of the inspiration of the Bible
receives yet another severe check when it is
pointed out that in Josh. ii. 9-13, even the
Canaanitish harlot Rahab uses four times this
name of Iaou, which is said to have been revealed
to the Israelites during the march even then not
concluded, and to have been allowed to be pronounced only by the Israelitish High Priest, and
by him but once a year.

As to the alleged inspiration of Genesis, it
is evident that, though re-written by Ezra or
some other Jew, the early part of same—*i.e.,*
the all-important commencement of the Bible
story—is Babylonian in origin. From the story
of the Creation to that of the Tower of Babel
the Bible is not Israelitish, nor Jewish, but
Babylonian.

To commence with, it is well known to those
acquainted with the remains of the Assyrian and
Babylonian civilisations, that the stories of the
Creation, the Temptation, the Fall, the Deluge,
and the Confusion of Tongues, were the common

property of the Babylonians centuries before the date of the alleged Exodus under Moses. At least one representation of the man, the woman, the tree, the fruit, and the serpent, has come to light ; and in this the hands of the woman are depicted as stretched out towards the forbidden fruit. The fragments which have survived the ages also contain references to a wicked serpent of night and darkness who brought about the fall of Man ; and at one and the same time show that ages before Moses the Accadians were in possession of the stories he is alleged to have been inspired to write, and also that those stories were in some cases, if not in every instance, more or less astronomical in origin and of an allegorical character.

As to Eden, this is found by students of the ancient cuneiform inscriptions to have been the name of the field or plain of Babylonia where, according to the old legends inherited by the Babylonians from a bygone age, the living creatures were created. The Jewish adapters have slightly altered the course of the four rivers or canals of the story, but these are still traceable

in the names ; for Pishon is the Babylonian name
for canal, and Gihon only a slightly corrupted
version of the Accadian name of the river by the
side of which Babylon was built ; and that the
Euphrates and Tigris were Babylonian rivers
does not need demonstration. As to the Tower
of Babel, the Babylonian origin of this particular
Bible story is too obvious to need pointing
out.

Even the word Sabbath is Babylonian. And
the observance of the seventh day as a Sabbath
or day of rest by the Accadians thousands of
years before Moses or Israel or even Abraham or
Adam himself could have been born or created,
is admitted by, among others, the Bishop of
Manchester. For in an address to his clergy
already mentioned, he let fall these pregnant
words :—

" Who does not see that such facts as these compel us to remodel our whole idea of the past, and that
in particular to affirm that the Sabbatical institution
originated in the time of Moses three thousand five
hundred years after it is probable that it existed in
Chaldæa, is an impossibility, no matter how many

Fathers of the Church have asserted it? Facts cannot be dismissed like theories." [1]

Such are some of the many facts which have to be assimilated ere one can be in a position to fairly judge as to the real origin, date, and nature of the Hebrew Scriptures.

---

[1] Visitation Charge, Blackburn, 1889.

CHAPTER V.

THE SUN-GOD IAOU (JEHOVAH).

L ET us now commence a brief survey of Old Testament history.

Even as early as the third chapter of Genesis clear traces of astronomical allegory and Sun-God worship are to be found ; for the statement that the seed of the woman should be bruised in the heel by the serpent, which in its turn should be bruised in its head, is very plainly a reference to the Zodiac, as will be shown later on.

The evidently astronomical basis of the stories of Enoch, of the Deluge, of Joseph's dream, of the twelve sons of Israel, and of the seventy-two descendants of Israel, has already been pointed out.

In Exod. xix. 18 we are told that Iaou descended upon Mount Sinai in fire.

In Exod. xxiv. we read that after an altar with twelve pillars had been built and burnt sacrifices offered, the four leaders and seventy-two elders of Israel went up the mount and saw the God of Israel. Here the seventy-two elders evidently represent the seventy-two years it takes for the Equinoxes to precess one degree, the four leaders the four quarters, the twelve pillars the twelve months, and the God of Israel the Sun. And what the Israelites went up to see was no doubt the Sunrise, for we are expressly told that it was "early in the morning."

We are also told that the glory of Iaou was like "devouring fire" (Exod. xxiv. 17).

It should here be pointed out that though the word Elohim is in the 11th, 16th, and 27th verses of Exod. xxxii. translated "God," it is carefully translated "gods" (with a small "g"), in verses 1, 4, 8, 23, and 31. The result is to create an entirely wrong impression upon the student of the Bible concerning the incident of the golden calf.

The story, as told in the original, is that the Israelites, during a prolonged absence upon the

part of Moses, said to Aaron, " Up, make us a
God which shall go before us "; that Aaron
demanded gold, and made with it a molten calf;
that Aaron, pointing to the calf, heifer, or bull,
then said, "This is thy God, O Israel, which
brought thee up out of the land of Egypt"; that
the High Priest, Aaron, built an altar before it
and proclaimed a feast to Iaou, and that Aaron
and the others offered burnt offerings to this calf,
heifer, or bull, as to a recognised representation
of Iaou.

It is true that Moses is said to have ground
the calf to powder as an affront to the second
of the commandments upon the tables of stone
he was bringing with him from the Mount; and
that, letting his brother Aaron go unpunished,
he made the children of Levi slay three thousand
men (verses 27, 28), and that, not content with
this, Iaou himself " plagued the people because
they made the calf which Aaron made" (verse 35).

But all this is plainly a fairy story. The facts
to be noted are that the first High Priest of Iaou
or Jehovah is declared by the Bible to have made
a representation of a calf, heifer, or bull; to have

proclaimed same to be a representation of Iaou ; to have built an altar to it, and sacrificed to it as if to Iaou ; and yet to have retained the High Priesthood of Iaou.

Needless to say, the golden calf, heifer, or bull, was a representation of the Sun-God in Taurus ; that is, the Sun-God of the Zodiac ; which, as we have seen, was planned when the Sun was entering the constellation in question.

In Numb. xxi. we are told that Iaou told Moses to make a serpent of brass ; and that whoever looked thereupon was saved. This is curious, as the second commandment forbade the making of any image, and Moses is previously represented as objecting to the golden calf because it was an image. The explanation of course is, that the ten commandments as narrated in Exodus were quite unknown till about a thousand years after Moses, as shown by the general acceptance by the Israelites of the calves erected by Jeroboam as representations of Iaou, and by the worship paid to a brazen serpent right down to the time of Hezekiah.

That this story of the brazen serpent, like that

of the golden calf, refers to the Zodiac, can need
no demonstration after what has already been
said.

In Numb. xxii. 41 we are told that Balak
took Balaam "up into the high places of Baal";
and in Numbers xxiii. 1-5, that Balaam had seven
altars built there, and sacrificed upon each a
bullock and a ram. The Bible also tells us that
after these burnt offerings to the Sun-God or
Baal, Elohim mét Balaam (verse 4), and Iaou put
a word in Balaam's mouth. In other words
Baal, Elohim, and Iaou, were but different names
or titles of the Sun-God.

As a matter of fact, even where later on in the
Bible Iaou and Baal are represented as opposing
deities, such representation is entirely due to the
fact that those who worshipped the Sun-God
under one name happened to be at variance with
those who worshipped him under the other.

In Josh. x. 12 we come to the significant
passage, "Then spake Joshua to" Iaou, "and he
said in the sight of Israel, *Sun*, stand thou still."
For this is plainly equivalent to saying that the
Sun and Iaou or Jehovah were one and the same.

This is still more clearly shown by verses
13, 14, where we read, "So the Sun stood still in
the midst of heaven, and hasted not to go down
about a whole day. And there was no day like
that before it or after it that" *Iaou* "hearkened
unto the voice of a man."

In 1 Sam. vi., we are told a story about the
Ark of Iaou, which is couched in very significant
terms. It is stated that when the Philistines,
who had captured the Ark, desired to know if
certain troubles which befell them were due to
their possession of the Ark of the God of the
Israelites, they put the Ark in a new cart and
harnessed two milch kine to same, and left the
milch kine to themselves, saying, "If it goeth up
by the way of his own coast to Beth-shemesh,
then he hath done us this great evil ; but if not,
then we shall know that it is not his hand that
smote us." And we are told that the kine left
their calves behind, and of their own accord, as it
were, went with the Ark of Iaou to Beth-shemesh,
and "turned not aside to the right hand or to the
left." Now, why the significance so evidently
attached to the fact that the Ark of Iaou not only

was taken by the milch kine to one of the towns
or villages of Israel, but was taken to this
particular place called Beth-shemesh? The
reason stares us in the face, for Beth-shemesh
means The House of the Sun.

From Beth-shemesh, the House of the Sun,
the Ark of Iaou was taken to Kirjath-jearim
(1 Sam. vi. 21); which also is significant. For
Kirjath-jearim was Kirjath-baal (Josh. xviii. 14),
the city of the Baal.

The Ark of Iaou remained at the city of the
Baal for some seventy years, for we are told that
when David removed it to Mount Zion after his
capture of Jerusalem from the Jebusites (1 Chron.
xi. 4), he and all Israel went to " Baalah, that is
to Kirjath-jearim, which belonged to Judah "
(1 Chron. xiii. 6), for it.

It is also noteworthy that King Saul named
one of his sons Esh-Baal, which signified "a man
of the Baal "; that Jonathan named his son Merib-
Baal, which signified "the Baal is contending";
and that King David himself named one of his
sons Baal-iada, "the Baal knows." This last
name is given as Beeliada in the Authorised

Version, but the Septuagint and other sources of information show that the Baal was referred to.

As to Solomon, when he sent to Hiram, King of Tyre, for the supplies of cedar wood requisite for the building of the Israelitish temple to Iaou, that kingly worshipper of the Baal is recorded as having " rejoiced " greatly, and said, " Blessed be " *Iaou*, " which hath given unto David a wise son." In other words, King Hiram deemed the Baal and Iaou one and the same.

As to the story of Solomon's " doing evil in the sight of Iaou," owing to the influence of his non-Israelitish wives, the Bible tells us that this lay in building a high place for Chemosh the Sun-God of Moab, and for Molech the Sun-God of Ammon. But no mention is made of his building one for the Baal, for the simple reason that the Baal was the Sun-God of the land and not a strange god. It is quite evident that Iaou was but a name for the Baal of Canaan. The Baal denounced by the prophets in later times was the Tyrian Baal, whose worship was introduced by Jezebel. And their anger even against the Tyrian Baal was due to the fact that this famous daughter of King Ethbaal of Tyre more or less ruined their profession by introducing hundreds of foreign priests.

The kingdom created by King David fell to pieces soon after the death of his son Solomon, despite the alleged promise of Iaou that it should continue for ever. The revolting ten tribes, as the larger number, were given the national name ; and their ruler, not that of those faithful to the royal line of David, was called King of *Israel.*

But although the leader of the larger host, Jeroboam, King of Israel, was at this great disadvantage compared with Rehoboam, King of Judah : the only Temple of Iaou was in the dominions of Rehoboam, and if the ten tribes still went up to Jerusalem to worship, that fact, and the remembrance of the glories of Kings David and Solomon, might cause them to become reconciled to the idea of being once more ruled by Rehoboam.

What was Jeroboam to do ? He took counsel, we are told, and erected a calf, heifer, or bull of gold at Bethel, and another at Dan ; and said, " It is too much for you to go up to Jerusalem ;

behold thy God " (not "gods," for this same word Elohim is elsewhere in this same chapter rendered " God," and Jeroboam only drew attention to one at a time, and both calves represented one and the same deity), "which brought thee up out of the land of Egypt " (i Kings xii. 28).

Now Jeroboam's plan succeeded. It is, therefore, evident that the golden calf, heifer, or bull, the well-known symbol of the Sun in Taurus, was recognised by the Israelites as a correct representation of the God worshipped at Jerusalem.

Years passed away, and although Jeroboam's line was wiped out of existence as a result of internal quarrels among the ten tribes, the Israelites showed no sign of wishing to re-unite with the two tribes or Jews, and the kingdom Jeroboam established at the expense of the House of David remained intact.

Eventually a soldier named Omri secured the throne. His son Ahab was fortunate enough to obtain in marriage the hand of Jezebel, the daughter of Ethbaal, King of Tyre, and this alliance doubtless added to the stability of the kingdom of Israel. It, at any rate, resulted in the founding of a dynasty.

But while this alliance gave to the line of Omri a prestige which the descendants of Jeroboam had lacked, and put Ahab above all other possible competitors for the throne of Israel, the Bible seems to hint that it placed the latter king in an awkward position. His future being perhaps more or less dependent upon the good-will of the princess he married, Ahab is said to have allowed Jezebel a power not often granted to queens in those days.

The Bible records that, as a result of marrying the daughter of the King of Tyre, Ahab went and served the Baal; that is, the Tyrian Baal. Also that Ahab, influenced by Jezebel, made what is wrongly translated as a " grove." This " grove " was an " asherah "; either an image of the Goddess Asherah, Ashtoreth, or Venus, or else a phallus, such as was used in the obscene rites attaching to the worship of that goddess.

Further on the Bible makes a series of statements which need careful consideration.

In 1 Kings xviii. 4 we are indirectly told that

Jezebel had all the priests of Iaou whom she
could capture killed ; for it is stated that when
she " cut off " the priests of Iaou, Obadiah saved
a hundred of them in a cave.

Elijah is, however, represented as having no
fear of King Ahab, and is stated not only to have
told Ahab's servant Obadiah to ask the king to
come and see him, but to have had an interview
without unpleasant results to himself, and even
to have persuaded King Ahab to summon " all
Israel "—and more especially the prophets of
the Tyrian Baal and of the goddess Asherah—
to meet him at Mount Carmel. This scarcely
agrees with the previous statement of the sentence of death upon all priests of Iaou.

Elijah is then represented as stating to the
multitudes which at the King's command assembled at Mount Carmel, that he alone remained
a prophet of Iaou.

Elijah, representing Iaou, as the *Canaanitish*
Baal or Sun-God was now called, and the four
hundred and fifty prophets of the Tyrian Baal,
are stated to have then built altars, and to
have entered into competition for a visible

sign of divine favour. Each side is said to
have laid wood upon its altar, and to have
sacrificed a bullock upon same, and then to have
appealed to God—*i.e.*, to the Sun-God—to answer
by fire. Fire is said to have fallen upon the
altar erected by Elijah, whereupon the prophet
of Iaou induced the people to surround the
prophets of the Tyrian Baal and let him murder
them one by one. King Ahab is said to have
looked on at this unmoved, and to have accepted
an invitation given by the red-handed Elijah,
to eat and drink with him directly after the
slaughter. (1 Kings xviii. 41.)

Notwithstanding all this, and the declaration of
the Israelites that Iaou was God, Elijah, the
friend of Ahab, is immediately afterwards
recorded as once more complaining that he only
was left of the prophets of Iaou. He asserts
that all save he were slain by the sword, and that
his life was sought. This does not agree with
the former statement that one hundred prophets
were saved by Obadiah. Nor can the assertion
be reconciled with the friendly terms upon which
he is said to have been with the king.

Moreover, we are told in 1 Kings xx. 13 of a prophet who came to Ahab in the name of Iaou, and whose advice the king took. Also in verse 28 of yet another prophet of Iaou whom Ahab deferred to. And, in verses 35-42, of yet another prophet of Iaou. This one, too, is said to have been recognised by the king as one " of the prophets."

And at the very end of Ahab's reign we find this king summoning the prophets of Israel, some four hundred in number, and asking their advice, whereupon they are represented as answering *in the name of Iaou.* (1 Kings xxii. 6.)

It is also noteworthy that Ahab and Jezebel named their daughter Athal*iah*, and their son Ahaz*iah*. Whether, therefore, they did or did not consider the Baal worshipped by the countrymen of Jezebel, and the Baal worshipped by the Israelites as Iaou, to be one and the same deity, the fact remains that in compounding their children's names they did not, as in " Ethbaal," make use of the word Baal, but, as in " Elijah," made use of the word Iaou.

As to the wrath of Elijah, it would appear that

it was all expended upon the priests and prophets of the Tyrian Baal, as no mention is made of his thundering against, or competing with, or slaying, the prophets of the goddess Asherah ; notwithstanding the obscene rites connected with her worship, and the fact that the prophets in question are said to have sat at Jezebel's table, or, in other words, to have been supplied with food and other necessaries by the queen in question.

Nor was Elijah's quarrel one with idolatry, for the golden calf erected at Dan and that at Bethel were undenounced by him, and, till they were carried away nearly two centuries later by Tiglath Pileser and Shalmaneser, remained the acknowledged representations of Iaou, and were till the end worshipped as such by the Israelites.

Taking all the contradictory statements of the Bible on these matters into account, such little residuum of apparent fact as can survive a close analysis seems to be this ; that a large number of priests of the Tyrian Baal accompanied Jezebel into her husband's kingdom, and that the priests of that Canaanitish Baal whom the Israelites worshipped as Iaou naturally objected to their profession being spoiled by the introduction of a large foreign element. And in self-defence the Israelitish priests and prophets declared the Tyrian conception of the Sun-God to be the enemy of the Israelitish Sun-God.

But it is clear that, whatever the quarrels of the priests and prophets, the subjects of Ahab and Jezebel one and all worshipped the Sun-God under some name or other. Even the mythical story of the fire from heaven falling upon the altar erected by Elijah and not upon that erected by the prophets of the Tyrian Baal, and of the consequent declaration by the assembled multitudes that Iaou was God, shows that at most the Israelites had but doubted which *was* the Sun-God.

And, as already stated, the golden calf, as erected at Dan and at Bethel, the symbol of the Sun in Taurus and of the Sun-God of the Zodiac, remained the unchallenged representation of the God of Israel right down to the time that the Assyrians carried both calves and ten tribes away, and they together vanished from the page of history.

But though we hear no more of the ten tribes or Israelites, we do of the two tribes or Jews. And it should be borne in mind that it is from descendants of the two tribes that we learn all we know concerning the ten tribes. The Old Testament comes to us, not from the Israelites, but from the Jews—from that small fraction of the descendants of the two tribes which gave up civilised Babylonia for devastated Canaan. It is therefore written, not from an Israelitish, but from a Jewish standpoint.

The Jewish chroniclers, writing centuries later, and after a somewhat similar calamity had befallen the Jews, ascribe the destruction of the Kingdom of Israel to the fact that the Israelites worshipped images, and the Baal ; that is, a foreign Baal. But the Jews themselves worshipped images ; and it was certainly no greater sin for the Israelites to worship the golden calf as a representation of Iaou, than for the Jews to worship a brazen serpent. And this, we know from their own admissions, they did till some time after the ten tribes were carried away.

That the Jewish chroniclers and prophets, when they referred to the Baal, meant a foreign Baal, and not the Baal or Sun-God worshipped throughout the length and breadth of the kingdoms of Israel and Judah, is clear from the fact that, though Elijah is represented as affirming that all the Israelites except himself had bowed down to the Baal, it is recorded in 2 Kings x. 18-28 that not long afterwards Jehu sent through all Israel proclaiming a solemn assembly for the Baal, and by stratagem got all the worshippers of the Baal *into one building*, surrounded them with soldiers, slew . them one by one, and thus for a time "destroyed Baal out of Israel."

In 2 Kings xviii. 4 we are told that Hezekiah, King of Judah, warned by the recent carrying away of the Israelites, tried to appease Iaou by destroying images, and by breaking in pieces the brazen serpent which the Jews worshipped in the temple at Jerusalem, the Jewish chronicler admitting that until those days his ancestors "did burn incense to it."

In 2 Kings xx. 1-11 we have what amounts

to an admission that Iaou was the Sun-God, the
recognised Baal of the land. For we are told
that Isaiah, in the name of Iaou, told Hezekiah
that he was about to die ; that in consequence
of a prayer of Hezekiah Iaou repented and sent
Isaiah again, this time to say that he would heal
Hezekiah, and that on the *third day* Hezekiah
would be able to go up to the house of Iaou to
return thanks ; that the king asked for a sign
that Iaou would heal him, so that on the third
day he would be able to go up into the house of
Iaou ; that Isaiah declared, " This sign shalt thou
have of Iaou, that Iaou hath spoken " ; that the
option of two signs was offered Hezekiah, one
that the Sun's shadow should go forward ten
degrees, the other that the Sun's shadow should
go back ten degrees ; and that Iaou brought the
shadow back ten degrees. In other words, the
shadow of *Iaou* is spoken of; and Iaou was
the Sun or Sun-God.

But the Jewish chronicler, writing as he did
after the Jews had been carried into Chaldæa
as captives, and had come into close contact with
the higher ideas of the nature of the Sun-God

held by the more civilised Babylonians and
Persians, tries here and elsewhere to hide the
self-evident fact that before his ancestors were
conquered by the Babylonians their Sun-God was
little better than a mere personification of the
physical Sun. We are accordingly told that
Josiah, King of Judah, who reigned long after the
ten tribes disappeared from the scene, and only
a few years before the two tribes were driven
away to Babylonia, commanded the High Priest
of Iaou to bring out of the temple of Iaou
all the vessels which were made for the Baal ;
and put down the black-robed priests of Iaou
whom the kings of Judah had ordained to burn
incense in the high places of Judah, unto the
Baal and the Sun, and the Moon, and the
Zodiacal Constellations, and the stars of heaven
(2 Kings xxiii. 5.) Also that Josiah took away
from the entrance of the house of Iaou the horses
which the kings of Judah had given to the Sun.
The admitted fact that the kings of Judah gave
statues of horses to the Sun, and placed them
at the entrance to the temple, however, tells a
tale. So also does the fact that not till Josiah

commanded the High Priest of Iaou to bring out
of the temple the vessels consecrated to the Baal,
is the High Priest or any other priest of Iaou
represented as objecting to the presence of such
vessels in the temple of Iaou.

How then does the Jewish chronicler account
for his statement that, while the priests of Iaou
had vessels consecrated to the Baal in the temple
of Iaou, and horses dedicated to the Sun at the
entrance to the temple of Iaou, it was left to a
youthful king to point out the errors of the spokes-
men of Iaou ? He does so in a very curious and
significant way. He alleges that the Book of
the Law was accidentally found ; that the king,
high priest, priests, and people, were all alike
astonished at its contents ; that they consulted
" Huldah the prophetess " ; and that upon her
saying it was the word of Iaou, the king set on
foot the reforms we have been considering.

Now, whether there be any truth in this story
of the Jewish chronicler or not, it is equivalent
to an admission that the ten tribes never had and
never heard of a Book of Moses, and that the two
tribes, even ninety years after the blotting out of

the ten tribes, were still ignorant of the existence of such a book.

This finding of the Book of the Law is said to have taken place in the eighteenth year of King Josiah, only some thirty or forty years before the Jews were carried away to Chaldæa as captives. Till then they evidently did not even keep the Passover (2 Kings xxiii. 21), and the chances are that this custom was one which they learned to observe when captives in Chaldæa, for even the names of the Jewish months are Babylonian, and we have proof that their stories of the Creation, the Temptation, the Fall, the Deluge, and the Tower of Babel, were derived from Babylon. Even the—perhaps invented—story of the finding of the Book of the Law before the captivity in Chaldæa, and of the acceptance of same by the priests of Iaou as the word of Iaou because a certain woman said it was the word of Iaou, is of itself sufficient demonstration that the Iaou or Jehovah of Judaism, who is a more or less spiritual Sun-God, and is represented as denouncing the making of graven images, is a conception of very late date, certainly never known to the ten tribes,

and probably attained to by the Jews as a result
of their captivity in Chaldæa, and of the subsequent two hundred years' government under the
suzerainty of the Zoroastrian Persians of such
few descendants of the two tribes as cared to
return to Canaan.   In fact, Judaism was neither
more nor less than Babylonian Sun-God worship
tempered by the more spiritual conceptions of
the Zoroastrians.   It was the natural result of
the successive contact of a comparatively uncultured race which worshipped that " Light of the
World " so universally revered as the Lord of
the Hosts of the Stars of the Sky, with such
civilisations as those of Chaldæa and Persia.

CHAPTER VI.

DIODORUS SICULUS, writing early in our era concerning the real or supposititious legislators of the various races of Mankind, tells us that :—

" Among the Jews Moses pretended that the God surnamed Iao gave him his laws." [1]

This seems to imply that the Jews were not the only race which knew of a God named Iao or Iaou.

Let us, therefore, having shown from the internal evidence of the Old Testament, that the Israelites, right down to the time when the Assyrians swept them from the page of history,

---

[1] Diod. Sic., I. 94.

and the Jews down to within half a century of the time when the Temple records were burnt and they themselves were driven as captives into Chaldæa, worshipped the Canaanitish Baal or Sun-God, now see if there is any external evidence concerning a God named Iao or Iaou, who may have been worshipped in other lands than that of Canaan.

First let it be noted, however, that there is in the British Museum a very ancient coin from Gaza, upon which is represented the Canaanitish Baal or Sun-God, and written over him, in old Phœnician characters, the word "Iaou."

That the word in question occurs upon Assyrian monuments as the name of a deity has already been pointed out. That deity seems to have been a Phœnician one. And the Phœnicians and Canaanites were one and the same people, as St. Augustine has borne witness.[1]

But little can be found—perhaps but little was allowed to survive—concerning this God Iao in such works as the Christian Church allowed to

---

[1] *Eposit. Epist. ad Rom.,* § 13.

come down to us. We learn, however, from Cedrennus, that—

"Iao is among the Chaldæans interpreted as meaning Intelligent Light in the Phœnician tongue, and Sabaoth as meaning Over the Seven Heavens, that is, the Creator God." [1]

Julian bears witness as follows—

"The Phœnicians, who were wise and skilful in divine matters, declared that the rays proceeding in all directions were the unmixed energy of the One Pure Intelligence itself." [2]

The testimony of Lydus is also important. In one place he writes—

"Sabaoth, the Creator:—for thus do the Phœnicians name the creative number." [3]

And elsewhere he tells us that—

"The Chaldæans call the God Dionysos 'Iao,' which in the Phœnician language means Intelligent Light. He is also often called Sabaoth, as Master of the Seven Heavens or Creator." [4]

---

[1] I. 296. [2] § 134. [3] iv. 98. [4] iv. 38.

This declaration of Lydus that the Chaldæans
called the Sun-God Dionysos or Bacchus "Iao"
is noteworthy, especially when we remember
that the Sun-God Adonis, and the Adonai translated Lord throughout our version of the Hebrew
Scriptures, seem to have been one and the same
deity. For Adonis and Dionysos were the same.
As Plutarch has told us—

"They think Adonis to be the same as Dionysos."[1]

The identity of the Canaanitish Baal, and of
Iao, Bacchus, Dionysos, and Adonis, with the
Hebrew Adonai or Iaou, is moreover borne out
by yet another passage to be found in the works
of Plutarch. For elsewhere this famous historian
says—

"Then, O Lamprius, do you include among the
unutterable things of the Hebrews our country's God
Dionysos? Trouble him not, replied Moiragenes, for
I as an Athenian can answer for you, and do say that
he (the God of the Hebrews) is none other. But the
greater part of the evidences to that effect can be

---

[1] *Sympos.*, iv. *qu.* v. 3.

told and taught only to those initiated with us into the full triennial solemnity." [1]

That the God Dionysos, whom Plutarch identifies with Iaou the God of the Hebrews, was the Sun or Sun-God, is well known. For instance, Macrobius tells us—

" In the following verse Orpheus declares the Sun to be Dionysos :—'Elios (*Helios*), whom men do surname Dionysos.' " [2]

Moreover, Labeo demonstrated that Iao, Father Bacchus, and Elios (*Helios*), the Sun, were one and the same.[3]

And Macrobius records the famous *Oracle* of Iao which emanated from the Temple of the Sun-God at Klarnos, in the following words—

" The Clarian Apollo having been asked which deity was the one to be called Iao, pronounced thus : It is but right that the Initiated should keep secret the ineffable mysteries, for prudence necessitates a certain measure of deceit on the part of the adroit mind. But it may be explained that Iao is the most

---

[1] *Sympos.* iv. 6.   [2] *Saturn.*, I. 18.
[3] *Concerning the Oracle.*

high God and above all others.   He is Aïdes (*Hades*) in winter and Zeus at the coming of spring-time, in the summer heat he is Elios (*Helios*), and at the close of autumn the tender Iao." [1]

At the Feast of Iaou, as the Feast of Tabernacles was called, the Levites were in the habit of shouting Hallelujah or Alleluia, *Praise-ye-Ia*, at frequent intervals.   It is a remarkable fact that at the triennial festival of Bacchus or Dionysos the same repeated cry of Ia was made, and that the Feast of Iaou or Feast of Tabernacles was neither more nor less than an exactly similar feast to that of the Sun-God Bacchus or Dionysos, and held at the same time of year as a thanksgiving for the corn, wine, and oil, secured in the harvest.   As Plutarch has told us—

" The time and manner of the greatest and most holy solemnity of the Jews are exactly the same as the holy orgies of Bacchus." [1]

We are told elsewhere of a very Bacchic practice of the Jews in connection with their Feast of Iaou—

---

[1] *Saturn.*, I. 18.   [2] *Symposiacs*, iv. 6.

" No less than one hundred and forty logs of wine were often used in the sacrifices." [1]

As to Hallelujah, Alleluia, or Praise-ye-Ia, this exclamation of the Hebrews seems to be merely an adaptation of the *Eleleu Ie* with which the ancient Greeks began and ended their hymns to the Sun-God Apollo. " Hallelujah " is placed in exactly the same way at the beginning and end of many of the Psalms, as was " Eleleu Ie " at the beginning and end of much older hymns to .Apollo.

There are reasons why this should remind us of the mystic symbol erected in the pro-naos of the Temple of Apollo at Delphi.

This renowned symbol has become known to fame as the " Golden E," and Plutarch wrote an essay upon it which is still extant.[2]

The real meaning of the mystic symbol was, as Plutarch has told us, unknown.

The classic writer in question had, however, five suggestions to offer: (1) that the symbol was the numeral 5, and represented the five sages

---

[1] *Menachoth*, xiii. 5.   [2] *Inscrib. forib. templi Delp.*

who presented it to the temple; (2) that it was EI = *if*, and referred to the fact that inquirers of the Delphic Oracle asked "if"; (3) that it was an abbreviation, EI, of EITHE = "*would that*," and was therefore a sort of invocation; (4) that it was the numeral 5 as a mystic number; and (5) that it meant "Thou art."

But (1) there were three of these symbols at the entrance to the temple of Apollo at Delphi, and though the one first placed there—the wooden one—was that reputed to have been given by certain sages, their number is sometimes given as seven, and from no point of view does this suggested meaning seem an adequate cause for the erection of this first symbol, and the later ones of similar shape ; (2) that it was in reality EI = "*if*," seems equally unlikely; (3) that it was an abbreviation of EITHE = " would that," is also improbable ; (4) it is not easy to see why the mystic numeral 5 should have been made so much of, and the mystic numerals 3, 4, 7, and 9, ignored ; and (5) that it meant "Thou art," though more likely, is certainly not proven by Plutarch.

As will have been seen, while some think the symbol in question—apparently a crescent, or nearly completed circle, pierced by a straight line passing from the right through the aperture to the opposite side—to have been a sort of mystic E, others took it as meant for EI.

That the symbol in question was, so far as letters were signified, a combination of the two letters E and I, seems probable enough. But why read same from left to right? The symbol was said to be an ancient one even before the time of Plutarch, and the oldest method of writing and reading was from right to left. Approaching the symbol in this direction we first come to the straight line, and arrive at what was probably the " hidden word "—viz. Ie,—the mystic Ie of the " Eleleu Ie," already referred to as akin to the Ia and Allelu*ia* of the Israelites.

The so-called E of the temple of Apollo at Delphi seems, however, to have been not so much the " hidden word " of a bygone age, as a Phallic symbol referring to the bi-sexual powers of the Creator.

As such the symbol or Ie of course signified

the "Self-Existing One," and it is noteworthy that this is exactly what the Jews who returned from Babylon declared the name of their God Ie or Ia to mean.

That the name of the Hebrew God was Ia, Iao, or Iaou, is moreover borne out by Irenæus, Origen, Epiphanius, Hesychius, Porphyry, and Clement of Alexandria; all of whom, in addition to the other ancient writers already mentioned as doing so (*e.g.*, Diodorus Siculus), testify that the Jewish God was called Iao.[1]

It is also worthy of mention that, contrary to the practice of the authors of the Gospels "according to" Matthew, Mark, Luke, and John, the author of the Gospel accepted by the Gnostics spoke of God as Iao.

As perhaps showing an additional reason for the hatred of Jezebel and others who tried to introduce into Canaan the worship of the Tyrian Baal or Sun-God, it may be well to note that there is much evidence to the effect that it was

[1] Irenæus, *Hæres*, ii. 66; Origen, *in Dan.* II.; Epiphanius, *Hær.* xx.; Hesychius, *in many places*; Porphyry, in Eusebius, *Præp. Ev.*, x. 11; Clement of Alexandria, *Strom.* v.

rather to the Tyrian Baal, whom the Greeks called Heracles, than to the Phœnician and Canaanitish Baal whom the Greeks called Adonis and the Israelites Adonai and Iaou, that human sacrifices were offered in days of old.[1]

Representations or symbols of Iaou were undoubtedly worshipped by the ten tribes right down to the time that they disappear from history, and by the two tribes at a yet later date. There appears, however, to have been a temple of Iao upon Mount Carmel, *not mentioned in the Old Testament*, in which that deity was worshipped without an image, and to which a monkish fraternity was attached. This fraternity was certainly not wholly Israelitish or Jewish, if indeed in any degree so; and it seems to have been spared when the Babylonians devastated the land, for we learn that at a later date than the deportation of the Jews to Chaldæa, Pythagoras stayed with the Monks of Iao at Carmel when studying the mysteries of the Sun-God

---

[1] Silius, *Ital.*, iv. 770; Lactantius, *Inst.*, i. 21; Eusebius, *de laud. Const.*, xiii.; Diodorus Siculus, xx. 14; Porphyry, *de Abst.*, ii.

Adonis, the headquarters of whose worship were
at the Phœnician city of Byblus, at the foot of
Lebanon.[1]

Now, the poor Jews who returned from Babylon
after two or three generations had been born and
bred in a far more cultured environment than
that of their ancestors, would naturally have
gained many ideas from their close contact with
higher civilisation, and, returning as they did to
a devastated land, would probably be influenced
not a little by such a fraternity as that of the
Monks of Iaô, who escaped the vengeance of the
Babylonians which so nearly visited the two
tribes with the oblivion which the Assyrians
meted out to the ten.   As the ancient writers lay
stress upon the fact that at this particular temple
of Iao, the one upon Mount Carmel to which this
monkish fraternity was attached, and all mention
of which is carefully omitted from the Scriptures
of the Jews, there was *no* image, it is clear that
it would also have been natural for these Monks

---

[1] Iamblichus, ii.; Tacitus, ii. 78 ; Clem. Alex., *Strom.* i. 304 ;
Suetonius, *Vespas.*

of Iao to teach the arriving Jews that the calamity which overtook their forefathers was due to the wrath of Iao or Iaou at the worship which they paid to images, representations, or symbols of deity. And seeing that the Monks of Iao's temple upon Mount Carmel had escaped when their ancestors were driven away as captives, the poor Jews who returned might not unnaturally be conceived to have accepted the theory in question.

Anyway, it will have been seen that the conclusions arrived at from an analysis of the historical works of the Old Testament—viz., that the Israelites from first to last, and the Jews almost, if not quite, down to the time that they were deported to Babylonia, worshipped the Canaanitish Baal or Sun-God as El, Elohim, Adonai, or Iaou ; and, moreover, worshipped him as the Sun, the Most High God outshining all the other lights of heaven ; that the God surnamed Iao or Iaou was not the God of the Israelites and Jews only ; and that the higher and more spiritual conception of Iaou held by the descendants of the Jews who returned from

Babylon was, like the Hebrew Scriptures then produced, partly annexed, partly evolved, and almost wholly assigned an utterly unreal origin and date—are not without extraneous evidence to support them.

CHAPTER VII.

THE ORIGIN AND DATE OF GENESIS.

REMEMBERING that the Bible itself admits that even as late as the accession of Josiah to the throne of Judah, about the year 640 B.C., and eighty years after the Israelites or ten tribes had been carried away, *there was no known copy of the Book of Moses in existence,* the " Book of the Law " (2 Kings xxii. 8), " Book of the Covenant " (2 Kings xxiii. 2), or " Book of the Law " of Iaou "given by Moses" (2 Chron. xxxiv. 14) being said to have been "found" in the reign of Josiah, and both King, Priests, and People to have been astonished at its contents (2 Kings xxii. 13, xxiii. 2 ; 2 Chron. xxxiv. 21, 22), and that the Temple and its archives were admittedly destroyed in the year 588 B.C. by the Babylonians, let us now briefly inquire into the date and origin of the earlier of the Scriptures which Christians annex from the descendants of such poor Jews as returned from Babylon, and call the Old Testament.

Two other dates should first be mentioned :— the return of some forty thousand Jews from Babylon about 536 B.C., and the rewriting of the sacred Scriptures by Ezra between the years 460 B.C. and 440 B.C.

Let us consult the Fathers upon the subject. Tertullian says—

" When Jerusalem was destroyed by the Babylonian storming, it is well known that every article of Jewish literature was destroyed, being afterwards restored by Ezra." [1]

Clement of Alexandria says—

" When the Scriptures had been destroyed at the Captivity by Nebuchadnezzar, Ezra, a Levite or Priest in the time of Artaxerxes, King of the Persians, having become inspired, reproduced prophetically all the ancient writings." [2]

---

[1] *De hab. mul.*, iii.   [2] *Strom.*, I. xxii. 49.

St. Jerome says—

" Whether you choose to say that Moses was the author of the Pentateuch, or Ezra the restorer of that work, I have no objection." [1]

St Irenæus says—

" Then, in the days of Artaxerxes, King of Persia, he inspired Ezra the priest of the tribe of Levi to set in order again all the words of the former prophets, and restore for the people the legislation of Moses." [2]

And St. Augustine says—

" Ezra restored the Law, which had been burnt by the Chaldæans in the Temple Archives, he being full of the same spirit which had been in the Scriptures." [3]

The Jewish historian Josephus is discreetly silent upon the point in question, simply assuming that the Law of Moses and other Scriptures were in possession of the Jews who remained at Babylon, quoting, as he does, an evidently fictitious letter of " Xerxes, king of kings," to " Ezra, the priest and reader of the Divine Law,"

---

[1] *Ad. Heb.*, iii.   [2] *Adv. hær.*, III. xxi. 2.
[3] *De Mir.*, II. 33.

directing him to go with other Babylonian Jews
"with those presents which I" (Xerxes) "and my
friends have vowed, with all that silver and gold
that is found in the country of the Babylonians
as dedicated to God, and let all this be carried to
Jerusalem, to God for sacrifices. . . . I grant all
that is necessary for sacrifices to God *according to
the Law.*"[1]

In the Second Book of Esdras or Ezra, however
—which Book has only this century ceased to
be printed as part of the English Bible, which
formed part of the Authorised Version of 1611,
and is still considered part of the Bible by the
authorities at Rome—we read as follows—

"Behold, Lord, I will go as Thou hast commanded
me, and reprove the people which are present: but
they that shall be born afterwards, who shall
admonish them? Thus the world is set in darkness,
and they that dwell therein are without light. For
Thy Law is burnt, therefore no man knoweth the
things that are done of Thee, or the works that shall
begin. But if I have found grace before Thee, send
the holy breath into me, and I shall write all that hath

---

[1] *Antiq.*, XI. v. 1.

been done in the world since the beginning which were written in Thy Law." [1]

Such is the evidence upon the subject. The only rational conclusion is the one already hinted at—viz., that there is nothing very old about the Old Testament considered as a collection of Jewish Scriptures ; what *is* old about the Old Testament being, not Jewish, nor Israelitish, but Babylonian.

---

[1] 2 Esdras xiv. 20-22.

CHAPTER VIII.

THE SUN-GOD OF THE NEW TESTAMENT.

PASSING on from the time when, some four and a half centuries before our era, Ezra, High Priest of the " Divine Law " at Babylon, was sent by the king to Jerusalem, and all the descendants of such captives as returned from Babylon some ninety years before assembling " with one accord " at that porch of the Temple which looked out towards the place of the Sun's rising,[1] produced and read the Law " according to " Moses before the assembled multitude, to the birth of Jesus, and, yet another century or so, to the time when followers of Paul produced the Gospels " according to " Matthew, Mark, Luke, and John—which attribute to Jesus a

---

[1] I Esdras ix. 38.

miraculous birth of a virgin, a proclamation by angels, a star which pointed out where He lay, a voice from heaven declaring Him to be God's Son, marvellous miracles, the raising of the dead, an ascension to heaven in bodily form, and other wonders equally unknown to Paul—let us now turn to the "New" Testament, cherished by followers of Paul, who, like the captives who returned from Babylon, worship towards the East, and, moreover, keep holy once a year, as did the Babylonians, a day dedicated to the Lord's Passover at the Vernal Equinox, and also, every week, the Roman Dies Soli, the Day of the Sun, the Lord's Day.

Before examining what followers of Paul declare to have been events in the history of "the Redeemer," let us first note that in an ancient Babylonian account of the Temptation and Fall which has been recovered, and is of far earlier date than the Jewish Scriptures, it is recorded that to the *Sun-God*, "their Redeemer," was appointed the fate of Man's first parents, who, thanks to the Serpent of Darkness, fell from their primal state of innocence and bliss through eating

fruit which had been forbidden them. The broken
tablet containing this account of what happened
at the beginning in the "garden of the Gods" is
now in the Koujounjik Gallery of the British
Museum.

As to the prophecy of the coming of the Sun-
God, which Christians profess to discover in that
particular version of the Babylonian legend of
the Fall which the Jews annexed as more or less
explaining the beginning of the human race and
the world's tragedy, let us analyse Gen. iii. 15,
the passage in question.

It runs : " I will put enmity between thee and
the woman, and between thy seed and her seed ;
it shall bruise thy head, and thou shalt bruise
His heel."

Now Christians cannot explain this reference
to the head of the Serpent of Darkness and to
the heel of the promised Redeemer. They do
not know why the Serpent is said to bruise the
heel of the Redeemer.

Yet the passage in question is clear enough to
those who hold the key. For in the Zodiac the
Serpent and the Sun-God are for ever pursuing

each other, and, as the Sun-God leads the way, the Serpent follows at his heels.

With the usual partiality of enthusiasts, who are seldom the most cultured members of a community, some who were more or less versed in the Zodiacal Cult, ignoring the fact that the precession of the Equinoxes which caused the Sun-God to move through the constellations towards Scorpio in time caused Scorpio to be no longer the Prince of Darkness, represented the Sun-God as gaining on the Serpent he pursued, and the Serpent as being still the Prince of Darkness, the former only of which is true. The fact of course is, that the Scorpion, or serpent, was so appropriate a name for the detested commencement of winter and of darkness, and therefore of evil in general and the Devil in particular, that, once established as the symbol for same, it could not be dislodged.

The Gospel "according to" Matthew commences with an alleged genealogy of Jesus the Nazarene, in which special stress is laid upon the statement that from Abraham to David, from David to the carrying away into Babylonia, and from the latter event to the birth of the Anointed, were each fourteen generations, various names being omitted from the list given in order to bear this out.

After this start, so big with promise of historical accuracy, the follower of Paul to whom we owe this Gospel traces the descent of Jesus from David through Joseph, and yet declares that Jesus was born of a virgin—an alleged marvel which Paul knew nothing about.

This alleged marvellous birth of Jesus is said to have been a fulfilment of a prophecy by Isaiah running, " Behold a virgin shall be with child, and shall bring forth a son, and they shall call His name Emmanuel, which being interpreted is, God with us " (Matt. i. 23). But the oldest manuscripts of Isaiah do not read " virgin " but " young woman." And the original is not " *shall* conceive " but " *is* with child "—*i.e.*, had already conceived. Moreover, it does not state that " they shall call " His name Emmanuel or Immanuel, but " thou shalt "; it being a command to King Ahaz to so call a child about to be born ; which child, as an encouragement to the king, Isaiah prophesied would be a boy, and therefore a sign of good luck. And Jesus was called—*Jesus.*

The fact that in the later versions of the Hebrew Scriptures, such as the Septuagint and Vulgate, the word signifying "young woman" has been altered into "virgin," is very significant.

The misrepresentation of Isaiah's reference to a young woman who at the time the prophet spoke was about to bear a child, thus given in the Gospel "according to" St. Matthew, is clear evidence of an attempt to connect a presumably real Jesus with the Sun-God, as an alleged incarnation of same. For at the commencement of our era and for some centuries before and after, the Sun-God, whether worshipped as Osiris, or Horus, or Bacchus, was represented as the Son of the Virgin, because at the birth of the Sun at the Winter Solstice the Zodiacal constellation upon the Eastern Horizon was the constellation Virgo.

In other Gospels Jesus is represented as being born in a stable, that stable being, according to some, in a cave. This is a reference to the fact that at the time of the birth of the Sun in those days the constellation directly under the earth was that of Capricornis, which was also called the Stable of Augeas. Hence the saying of the Fathers that the Christ came as a second Hercules to clear out the Stable of Augeas.[1]

Caves were regarded as representations of the dome or vault of heaven ; and Sun-worshippers assembled in caves, and used same as temples, partly for that reason. The Stable of Augeas was therefore said to be in a cave.

We are told that Magi came from the East, in search of a King whose star they had seen in the East ; and that the star went before them and stood over where the young child was, pointing Jesus out to them as the King of kings. Christians say that these Magi were three kings, and that their names were Melchior, Gaspar, and Baltassar. In fact, Christians discovered the bodies of these three kings, and placed them in their cathedral in New Rome.

From Constantinople the bones of the three kings were, as a special favour to Milan, allowed to be moved to that city. When Milan was

---

[1] *Vide* Justin Martyr, *Dialog. cum Trypho.*

captured by Frederick Barbarossa A.C. 1162, the
Archbishop of Cologne persuaded that Emperor
to transfer the relics in question to his own
cathedral; and there for the last seven centuries
the bones in question have rested, the shrine of
the Three Kings being one of the greatest treasures
of the grand cathedral of Cologne.

But, the bones notwithstanding, it is all a fairy
story. Christians do not even know where the
bones were discovered, much less which were
the kingdoms the three kings ruled. Nor can
they explain how a star could have stood over
where the young child was, or have distinguished one child, or one building, or one
village, or one district, or even one country,
from another.

The fact is, that not earthly kings and
kingdoms are referred to, but the kingdom of
heaven, its King of kings, and its lesser kings.

Now if of a clear evening about the commencement of a new year we look Eastward, we see
the most glorious of all the constellations mount-
ing the sky. And the three stars so conspicu-
ously set together in Orion's belt are pointing

downwards to the East from which they came as if signifying the advent of a marvel.

And the marvel comes. For in a direct line with those three stars, Sirius, the brightest of all the Host of Heaven, is soon seen rising in the East.

Now the Egyptians used to set their Calendar by the heliacal rising of Sirius, and the Dog Star was accordingly known as the Herald of the Sun. And the old name given to the three stars in the belt of Orion was that of "the three Kings." It was therefore true that the three Kings had "seen His star in the East," the herald proclaiming the advent of the King of kings.

The day allotted to Jesus in the Christian Calendar as birthday or name day, is what was at the time Midwinter Day, the day of the Winter Solstice; that allotted to John the Baptist being Midsummer Day, the day of the Summer Solstice. In fact, Jesus represented the Sun in ascension, and the summer produced by its return from the South; his cousin, the Sun in declension, and the winter caused by its return to the South.

This is the real reason why John the Baptist

is represented as declaring that while he baptised with water Jesus would baptise with holy wind or breath ("the Holy Ghost") and fire (Matt. iii. 11). For Jesus did not baptise with fire. The rains of winter, and the warm winds and ripening heat of summer, are referred to ; and not the real but the allegorical Jesus.

In the same way, and in that way only, can the mystic saying also attributed to John the Baptist, " He must increase but I must decrease " (John iii. 30), be rationally interpreted. For this is a reference to the fact that days begin to lengthen at the Winter Solstice, and to shorten at the Summer Solstice.

We are repeatedly told that Jesus had *twelve* disciples. The reason why His chosen band is represented as never either less or more than twelve is evident. They are allegorical figures representing the twelve Mansions of the Sun and the corresponding twelve Months of the Year.

In the tenth chapter of the Gospel " according to " St. Luke another band of disciples is mentioned. Their number is mentioned twice, in

verses 1 and 17 ; and, as already pointed out,
though given in the Authorised Version as
seventy, was originally stated to have been
seventy-two. Even to-day the number is given
as seventy-two in the *Codex Vaticanus* and the
Codex Bezœ in both verses. This band of
seventy-two disciples represents that key to
heavenly knowledge, the number of years it takes
for the Sun-God, the place of the Sun at the
Vernal Equinox, to precess one degree of the
celestial circle.

The Bible gives us a glowing account of the
mission entrusted to these seventy-two disciples—
how Jesus sent them to every city " whither He
Himself would come," how they returned again
with joy saying that even the demons were
subject unto them, and how Jesus told them to
rejoice because their names were " written in
heaven." Those names may have been written
in heaven ; but they are not mentioned in the
Bible. And the mystic seventy-two are never
referred to again, comment upon which fact
would be superfluous.

In the seventeenth chapter of the Gospel " according to" Matthew we are told that Jesus took three of His twelve disciples up a high mountain, " And was transfigured before them : and His face did shine as the Sun, and His raiment was white as the light." Another account of the same alleged marvel is given in the Gospel "according to" Mark. Now the word given in English versions of the New Testament as "transfigured" is the Greek word usually translated as "metamorphosed." And to say that Jesus was metamorphosed, and His face did shine as the Sun and His raiment glisten like the light of the Sun, is as near as the teller of the story could go to hinting to those well versed in the lore of the kingdom of heaven, that Jesus was an allegorical representation of that king of heaven—the Sun.

In the Gospel "according to" Luke we are told that at the death of Jesus there was " a darkness over all the earth " for three hours, the Sun being eclipsed. No such eclipse of the Sun occurred, and this alleged marvel is merely another sign of the allegorical nature of the hero of the story.

The Gospel " according to " John begins by

telling us that " In the beginning was the "
Logos ; and that the Logos was " The true Light
which lighteth *every* man that cometh into the
world," whether believer or unbeliever, good, bad,
or indifferent.   Now the real Jesus was not, and
is not, such a light ; but the Sun was, and is.

As the Logos or Word was a philosophical
conception like the Idea of Plato, it more or less
represented Reason.   There is therefore some
likelihood that the author of this Gospel, following
in the footsteps of Paul as that famous Propagan-
dist did in those of the great Jewish philosopher
Philo, attempted to reconcile the Sun-God worship so universal in those days with the conceptions of the philosophers, and looked upon
the Logos as the Sun of the Soul, which Reason
may of course be said to be.   In fact, this Gospel
may be said to have rounded off the efforts of the
followers of Paul to popularise the ideas of the
philosophers and to transmute worship paid to
more or less physical conceptions of the Sun-God
into worship paid to a more spiritual conception,
which conception was allegorically said to have
been made flesh and to have dwelt with men,

because the Logos or Word—*i.e.*, Reason—was incarnate in Man.

It should be mentioned, too, that it is in the Gospel "according to" John that we have the account of Jesus turning water into wine. This is an evident allusion to the ripening power of the Sun's rays, without which no wine could be produced.

The miraculous draught of fishes, the increase of the loaves and fishes, the healing of the sick, the raising of the dead, and every other miracle attributed to Jesus, are, it should be noted, allegorical representations of the powers of the Sun. No miracle is mentioned which could not be included in such a category.

In John iii. 13 occurs the mysterious declaration, "And no man hath ascended up to heaven, but he that came down from heaven, even the Son of man which is in heaven." But this is mysterious only to those not aware that by the Son of man is figured forth the Sun which shines on men.

This should be clear to the reader, for Jesus was a Jew who presumably believed that at least two men, Enoch and Elijah, had ascended into heaven. And, be it noted, it is not alleged that Jesus had then done so. The words could therefore most certainly not have been uttered by a real Jesus, but are put in His mouth as a personification of the Sun-God who once a year comes down from heaven to be born and then ascends the heavens again, but is nevertheless all the time " *in heaven* "; just as the Son of man is expressly said to have been at the time this saying is said to have been uttered by a Jesus who was then upon earth, and therefore could not have been the Son of man.

In John v. 35 Jesus is represented as saying concerning His cousin John the Baptist, " He was a burning and a shining light: and ye were willing for a season to rejoice in his light." This is allegorically written of the Sun in declension, which John has already been shown to represent.

In John viii. 12 Jesus is represented as saying, " I am the Light of the world." Now despite all the preaching of the last nineteen centuries, Jesus is by no means the light of the world even yet. Of all the countless millions who have passed away since the commencement of our era, not one in a dozen has in any sense of the word had Jesus for his or her light. But the Sun-God was, and is, the Light of the *World*. Whether we conceive the Sun-God to be a personification of the powers of the Sun, or, like the philosophers, deem him to be the Logos of the All-Father, the Sun-God is undoubtedly the Light of the World. For the blessings of sunshine and of reason are showered broadcast by heaven, and are in every sense worldwide. Neither race, nor rank, nor creed, can monopolise them.

In John ix. 4, 5, Jesus is represented as saying, " I must work the works of Him that sent Me while it is day : the night cometh when no man can work. *As long as* I am in the world I am the Light of the world." All this demonstrably refers to the Sun and not to a real Jesus. Nor would it have been true of Jesus if He had been God incarnate, for in that case He would not have been pressed for time. Where the Sun works, it is day; and therefore, where 'tis day the Sun works. Note, too, the admission that only during the day, only while in the world, was this allegorical being the Light of the World.

Jesus is represented as explaining the last quoted saying by remarking, " Yet a little while is the light with you ; walk while ye have the light, lest darkness come upon you. While ye have the light, believe in the light." This further declaration that the light of the Christ was not a constant light, but, like that of the Sun, one not always present, still more clearly shows that the Sun—*i.e.*, the light of the Sun—is referred to.

And, finally, it is worthy of note that the writers of the Gospels did not once refer to the Christ as the " *Good* Shepherd." The adjective they used was not the Greek word signifying "good," but the Greek word signifying "beautiful."

Now, whom did the writers of the Gospels refer to when they wrote concerning the " Beautiful " Shepherd ? This much, at least, is certain ; that Apollo the Beautiful was known as the Shepherd long before our era, and that the Early Christian representations of the Christ as a Shepherd were copies of pre-Christian representations of Apollo as a Shepherd.

It stands proven that the Jesus of the New Testament was made the central figure of an allegory in which He was adorned with the attributes of the various conceptions of the Sun-God.

CHAPTER IX

M AN has ever worshipped the Rising Sun. It was only natural that he should do so. And in more senses than one has he always done so.

Even astronomically speaking, Man has ever and most naturally worshipped the rising Sun in more than one sense. For as there are two revolutions of the Earth, one around its axis and one around the Sun, there are of necessity two risings of the Sun—a daily one and an annual one. The daily rising turns night into day, and the yearly rising turns winter into summer.

Only in the Polar Regions is no daily rising visible, and only in the Equatorial Regions is no yearly rising visible.

At sunrise upon the day of the Passover or

Vernal Equinox, the two risings of the Sun are combined. Or, more correctly speaking, at the first sunrise after the time of the Vernal Equinox. Whether on the same day, or the next, might depend upon which of several modes of reckoning days is referred to. Also upon which century is referred to, as the time of the Vernal Equinox is affected by the precession of the Equinoxes.

Remembering these things, and also the notable traces of Sun-God worship which, as has been shown, exist in the Christian Gospels, let us now pass on to consider the general question of Sun-God worship in the days of the Fathers—*i.e.*, in the days when the followers of Paul, combining in one the almost universal belief in a Sun-God of some description, and the philosophic conception of a Logos or Word of God, fabled that both had become incarnate in the person of a famous Jewish teacher, and started a religion which, thanks to the patronage of the Sun-God worshipper Constantine, ultimately became the State religion of the Roman Empire.

As introducing the subject, let us first institute a comparison between certain striking features in the mode of worship in the Israelitish Temple of Iaou at Jerusalem, and others in practices of the Christian Church.

The Israelites of old, following the example of other Sun-God worshippers, built their Temple with its chief gate looking out towards the East. Their Temple was, in fact, oriented with care from the very first ;[1] and its eastern portal faced the true East, the place of the Sun's rising at the Vernal and Autumnal Equinoxes.

As might have been expected in a Temple erected to the Sun-God, the morning service in the one at Jerusalem, with the accompanying sacrifice of the Lamb of God, took place at Sunrise.

Upon the day of the Passover or Vernal Equinox, however, there was a special service which began even earlier, as upon that day the " Glory of the God of Israel" (Ezek. xliii. 2)— or, in other words, the direct rays of the Sun— entered the sanctuary ; and much had to be done before Sunrise.

---

[1] Josephus, *Antiq.*, viii. 4.

Sun-God temples were not only, for the most part, oriented to the place of Sunrise at the time the Sun crossed the Equator, but also built in such a way that only at Sunrise at the time of the Autumnal or Vernal Equinox could the rays of the Sun enter into the Holy Place. The fact that if the rays of the Sun could enter into the Holy of Holies at sunrise at the time of the Vernal Equinox they could also do so at Sunrise at the time of the Autumnal Equinox, seems to have been more or less ignored ; as also the fact that, as it is only at age-long intervals that in any given latitude the Sun can rise exactly at the time of its passing over the Equator, the rays which could penetrate one morning could possibly do so the next morning also—*i.e.*, two days in succession ; the allowance made, when building a temple, for the fact that the time of the Passover and time of Sunrise did not coincide, naturally taking effect in two directions. The exact effect of the allowance made would of course depend upon at what period of a given age the temple being considered was built, how long after the building was the epoch under consideration, and for how long a

time it was originally arranged that the rays of
the Sun should be able to enter the Holy of
Holies.

Some Sun-God temples, unlike the one at
Jerusalem, were arranged so that the rays of
the Sun could only penetrate into the Sanctuary,
not at the Equinoxes, but at either this or
that Solstice, preferably of course the Summer
Solstice. But whichever the plan adopted, the
idea and purpose were the same. The conception was that of the Sun-God visibly entering his
Temple once a year, the object that of impress-
ing the people with the prescience and power of
the priests.

In most countries the astronomer-priests seem
to have arranged it so that the rays once a year
allowed to penetrate into their Holy of Holies
should fall upon and illuminate an image of the
Sun-God; and the fact that the priests knew
exactly when the Sun-God was thus going to
manifest his presence could not fail to impress
the ignorant and credulous.

But the Israelitish priests hit upon an even
more ingenious way of increasing their hold upon

the imaginations of the people. They arranged that the rays in question should fall upon the High Priest himself, as, arrayed in his robes covered with precious stones representing the Sun and the twelve constellations, he stood facing the Eastern Portal, and the congregation looked westwards at him. As Josephus has told us, the jewels the High Priest wore "shined out when God was present."[1]

It is curious, too, to note that Josephus adds the remark, "This breastplate and this sardonyx left off shining two hundred years before I composed this book." This was put down to the displeasure of God at the transgressions of the people, but was no doubt due to the effects of precession. Why the matter was not put right when Herod's temple was built in place of that erected by such of the Jews as returned from Babylon, is a matter of conjecture, as the third temple was oriented as well as the first and second temples. Either the priests did not like to fable that God had returned to His temple,

---

[1] *Antiq.*, III. viii.

while the fact that their land was ruled by strangers showed that He was displeased; or, despite the fact that their new temple was oriented, they wished the real origin of the national religion to be forgotten, and the higher conception of the Deity as a purely spiritual being generally accepted.

As cloudy mornings occur sometimes even in the latitude of Jerusalem, there were times in days of old when the Sun-God did not make his expected entrance into his temple at the time of the Passover Sunrise. As Josephus says: "Moses left it to God to be present at his sacrifices when He pleased; and, when He pleased, to be absent."[1]   The priests were of course always ready with an explanation, and turned the "anger" of the Sun-God, as manifested every now and then by refusal to come into his temple, to good account.

Now it is true that while the majority of Christians pray towards the East, the Jews used to pray towards the West.   But this praying

---

[1] *Antiq.*, III. viii.

towards the West was arranged by the priests
so that the congregation might see the rays of
the Sun-God single out and illumine his vice-
gerent upon earth, the High Priest. The High
Priest looked eastward, through the opened
eastern portal, at the "Glory of the God of
Israel."

It is also worthy of passing note that Psalm
cxxxii. 7, 8, should be translated, "We will come
into His dwelling: we will worship toward the
place where Thy feet stand. Arise, O Iaou, into
Thy resting-place." As the rays which penetrated
the Holy of Holies fell upon the High Priest
as he looked eastward, the place "where Thy
feet stand" not improbably refers to that part of
the surrounding country first illumined by the
rays of the rising Sun as seen by him.

It is noteworthy, too, that Ezekiel prophetically
relates seeing the "Glory of the God of Israel"
come into His temple "by the way of the
gate whose prospect is towards the East." (Ezek.
xliii. 4.)

That this God of Israel, surnamed Iaou, was
the Sun-God, and His "glory" the rays of the

Sun, is clear from the fact that Ezekiel expressly says, not only that the said "glory" came from the East, but also that it illuminated the whole Earth. ·

It is also worthy of mention that Psalm lxvii. 32 (*Sept.*) calls upon men to sing unto Iaou who "In the east ascends to highest heaven."

As connecting Judaism and Christianity, Iaou and Jesus, it may be here remarked that the origin of the prophecy by Zechariah, spoken of Iaou the Sun-God, but alleged to have been spoken of a more earthly "Christ" or Saviour, of a personal Messiah, and—by Christians—of Jesus : "His feet shall stand in that day upon the Mount of Olives, which is before Jerusalem on the East" (Zech. xiv. 4), is a clear reference to the fact that as the High Priest looked out through the eastern portal of the temple for the first rays of the rising Sun at the time of the Passover, he looked out at the Mount of Olives, and the rays of Iaou first set foot upon that Mount. In fact, the Priest who had to sacrifice the red heifer to Iaou had to do so upon the Mount of Olives, and to do so, moreover, in a line with the altar and the true East ; for he had to sacrifice it upon that one spot upon the Mount of Olives whence he could see right through the eastern portal of the temple up to the sanctuary itself and the altar where the lamb of God was daily sacrificed.

For the same reason as the foregoing, Jesus is said to have "ascended" from the Mount of Olives. It was thence that the High Priest in the sanctuary saw laou ascend out of his sight.

The idea that, reversing the practice of the Jews, Christians have from the first placed their altars at the East end of their sacred buildings, is quite erroneous. The churches erected by the Christians of the first few centuries of our era were erected indifferently as to whether the altar was at the East or West end, so long as the edifice was built due East and West. For instance, Paulinus Nolanus tells us of a Christian Church, the altar of which was in the West,[1] while Socrates tells us that the Christian Church at Antioch where the Christians were first called

---

[1] *Ep.* 12, *ad Sever.*

Christians, was so built, [1] and Eusebius tells us
that the entrance of the Christian Church at Tyre
faced the rising Sun. [2] And though the above
instances are not given in his invaluable *History
of Architecture*, Dr. Ferguson says that " The
practice of turning the altar towards the East
was never introduced into Italy." [3]

This statement of Dr. Ferguson is a little too
sweeping an one. It is, however, well known
that a large number of Italian churches have
their altar at the West and the grand portal
towards the East ; so that the priests officiating
at the altar *could* look beyond the congregation
towards the place of the Sun's rising at the
Passover or Vernal Equinox. And it is noteworthy that both the present Cathedral of
St. Peter at Rome and the preceding St. Peter's
were so built. As has been pointed out regarding
Old St. Peter's—

" So exactly due East and West was the Basilica
that, on the Vernal Equinox, the great doors of the

[1] v. 22.   [2] *Ec. Hist.*, x. 4.
[3] *Ibid.*, 2nd Edition, iv. 58.

porch of the quadriporticus were thrown open at
sunrise, and also the Eastern doors of the Church
itself, and as the Sun rose, its rays passed through
the outer doors, then through the inner doors, and
penetrating straight through the nave, illuminated the
High Altar." [1]

The fact that, even to-day, the chief temple of
Christianity is built so that the rays of the Sun-
God could at sunrise on the day of his Passover
or Crossover of the Equator penetrate into the
Holy of Holies, is most significant.

So also is the fact that Christian Churches in
lands which lie to the east of Jerusalem—say
those of the Greek Church in the eastern half
of Asiatic Turkey—point, like those of western
countries, to the East, and not to Jerusalem or
any other earthly site.

Nor is this all; for as if Christians were at
heart aware it is only allegorically that the Bible
speaks of the Christ at some future date again
standing upon the Mount of Olives, the Christian
dead, even in countries to the east of Palestine,
are laid to rest with their feet towards, not the

---

[1] *The Builder*, January 2nd, 1892.

Mount in question, but the place of sunrise at the Vernal Equinox.

Partly because Christianity spread northwards into colder and cloudier climes, but chiefly, no doubt, because of the adoption from the Eleusinian or other mysteries of the doctrine of Transubstantiation (the actual presence of the Sun-God or Saviour of Mankind in the necessaries of life produced as a result of the rays emanating from him, consecrated samples of which necessaries came to be kept in every church and more or less worshipped), the practice of having the altar at the East gradually became the favoured one, for the Host was of course kept at that end as being nearest to the place of the Vernal Equinox.

Having shown that the Jews would naturally speak of the Sun-God as setting foot upon the Mount of Olives, when speaking of his return to his temple at Jerusalem, while we know Christians to have so spoken of Jesus, let us now proceed to examine the way in which the Fathers spoke of the Sun-God, and of his Adversary the Prince of Darkness.

Speaking of the initiation of Christians, who,

when initiated, were spoken of in early times as
" illuminated," St. Jerome says—

" In our mysteries we first renounce him that is in
the West, who dies to us with our sins : and turning
about to the East we make a covenant with the Sun
of Righteousness, and promise to be his servants." [1]

Now " Sun of Righteousness " is a term derived
from the last chapter of the last Book of the
Old Testament, certain words in the original text
of which are usually so translated. But the
meaning of the original is " the righteous Sun."

The Authorised Version of Malachi is very
misleading from first to last. For instance, the
" shall be " thrice repeated in verse 11 of the
first chapter, represents an original which means
" is "; and this completely leads one astray.
The fact is, this last of the prophetical messages
to the Jews is a complaint in the name of their
Sun-God Iaou that the Jews no longer worshipped
Iaou the Sun-God zealously, but offered blind and
lame animals upon his altar, *and treated him worse
than non-Jewish nations did.* Malachi i. 10-12

---

[1] *In Amos* vi. 14.

should be translated, " I have no pleasure in you, saith Iaou of the hosts of heaven, neither will I accept an offering at your hand. For from the rising of the Sun until the going down of the same My name *is* great among other nations, and in every place incense *is* offered unto My name, and a pure offering : for My name *is* great among the other nations, saith Iaou of the hosts of heaven ; but *ye* have profaned it."

The meaning of Mal. iv. 1, 2, referred to by St. Jerome, is equally clear when properly translated. For instance, " The day that cometh shall burn them up, saith Iaou of the hosts of heaven, that it shall leave them neither root nor branch. But unto those that fear My name shall the righteous Sun arise with healing in His wings," is evidently a prophecy that though Iaou the Sun-God would one day rise to destroy those who despised him, he would rise with healing in his wings for those who paid heed to the exhortations of the writer.

The key to the Book of Malachi and its alleged prophecies of Jesus lies in the fact that the writer in chapter i. verse 11, stated that, while the Jews were beginning to despise the Sun-God, that deity was held in the highest honour by the other nations, and incense was offered him in every land. The Sun-God is clearly the deity referred to ; for it was he who was then worshipped in every land, he whose name from the rising of the Sun unto the going down of the same was held great in every clime.

As Sun-God worship died out among the Jews, and their conception of Iaou evolved into that now held by them, the prophecies ceased. And it is not the Jews but the Christians who assert that those prophecies were fulfilled in Jesus, not Jews but Christians who are the Sun-God worshippers of to-day.

Further evidence that the Fathers thought of the Christ as " the righteous Sun," and of the Devil with his barbed tail as the Scorpion which stings with its tail and is in the Zodiac the symbol of the Adversary of the Sun-God, can be found in the words of St. Ambrose—

" When you entered into the baptistery and viewed your enemy whom you were to renounce, you then

turned about to the East.   For he that renounces the
Devil is turned unto the Christ." [1]

Cyril of Jerusalem is still more explicit·
Addressing the "illuminated" he says—

" You were first brought into the ante-room of the
baptistery and placed toward the West in a standing
posture, and then commanded to renounce Satan. . . .
The West is the place of Darkness, and Satan is
Darkness and his strength is in Darkness.   For this
reason ye symbolically look toward the West when ye
renounce the Prince of Darkness." [2]

Jesus, or, to be more accurate, the Anointed
One, was frequently spoken of by the Early
Christians as the Orient Light.   And they were
even taught to spit towards the Occident to show
their detestation of his Adversary the Prince of
Darkness ; their detestation, that is, of the
Serpent or Scorpion who in Zodiacal days ruled
over that Mansion of the Sun and corresponding
Month of the Year in which the Autumnal
Equinox took place, thus ushering in winter and

[1] *De. Mysteriis,* ii.   [2] *Il. Catech.,* 19.

all its horrors, and being generally regarded as the Opponent of the Prince of Light, the Sun-God at the Vernal Equinox ushering in the summer and ruling over the summer half of the year ; as the Scorpion, or Devil—*i.e.*, Evil One—with barbed tail, did over the six winter months when the Sun was in the "bottomless pit" of the South.

Passing on from the subject of orientation, it ought not to be overlooked that the worship of the Persian conception of the Sun-God was preached throughout the Roman Empire about the same time as Christianity, and that Tertullian admitted that the learned in his day considered Mithraicism and Christianity identical in all but name. Now Mithraicism is known to have met with great success even in Rome itself, and in Roman relics dedicatory inscriptions to "Deo Soli Invicto Mithrae" are frequently to be met with.

Even as early as the middle of the second century of our era we find the cult of Mithras of such importance that the Emperor Commodus decided to be initiated into its mysteries, and

become a "Soldier of Mithras."[1]   As the Zend-
Avesta declares Mithras the Sun-God to be the
First Emanation of Ormazd—*i.e.*, the First
Begotten of the All-Father and the manifestation
of that All-Father unto the world, or in other
words the Logos or Word of God by whom all
things were made—it is easy to see how, half
a century or so later, Commodus's successor
Constantine—whose patron God was Apollo
the Sun-God, and who retained upon his coinage
after he established Christianity as the State
Religion of the Roman Empire a representation
of the Sun with the inscription " To the invincible
Sun my companion "—came to recognise the title
Christ as but another name for the Sun-God.

So great was the likeness of Christianity to
Mithraicism that we find one of the Fathers
writing as follows—

"The Devil, whose business it is to prevent the
truth, mimics the exact circumstances of the Divine
Sacraments in the mysteries of idols. He himself
baptises same, that is to say, his believers and

---

[1] Lampridius.

followers; he promises forgiveness of sins from the sacred fount, and thereby initiates them into the Religion of Mithras: thus he marks on the forehead his own soldiers: there he celebrates the oblation of bread: he brings in the symbol of the resurrection, and wins the crown with the sword." [1]

Another of the Fathers, and one who wrote at an even earlier date, tells us that—

" The apostles, in the commentaries written by themselves which we call gospels, have delivered down to us how that Jesus thus commanded them : ' He having taken bread, after that He had given thanks, said, Do this in commemoration of Me ; this is My body : also, having taken the cup and returned thanks, He said, This is My blood ' ; and delivered it unto them alone. Which things the evil spirits have taught to be done out of memory in the mysteries and ministrations of Mithras." [2]

As Mithraicism was in existence before Jesus is said to have been born, and the rite of the Eucharist formed part of even other mysteries centuries before our era, this reference to " evil spirits " and " memory " is almost funny.

---

[1] Tertullian.   [2] Justin Martyr, *Apol.* ii.

Another noteworthy point is that the Gnostic Christians, who worshipped the Hebrew God under the name Iao, adored the same deity as Mithras—*i.e.*, the Sun-God.

This is clear from the fact that while one Father tells us that—

" Basilides made out that the number of the heavens was three hundred and sixty-five, the number of days in the solar year. Hence he used to glorify a Sacred Name, as it were, viz., the word Abraxas or Abrasax, the letters in which name, according to the Greek computation, make up that number," [1]

another of the Fathers writes—

" As Basilides, who called Almighty God by the portentous name of Abraxas, and says that the same word, according to the Greek numerals and the sum of his annual revolutions, are contained in the circle of the Sun; whom the heathen, taking the same sum but expressed in different numerical letters, call Mithras, and whom the simple Iberians worship under the names Lord Sun (*Baal Samus*) and Son of the Lord (*Bar Belus*)." [2]

---

[1] St. Augustine.   [2] St. Jerome.

This reference to the fact that each sign of the Greek Alphabet had a double significance, in that it represented a number as well as a sound—the signs called alpha, iota, and rho, for instance, representing 1, 10, and 100, as well as *a*, *i*, and *r*—and were figures as well as letters, should remind us that among the many names applied to the Sun-God in ancient days the most sacred seems to have been a word of three letters of the numerical value of six hundred and eight. As perhaps the most learned of the writers of the fourth century of our era wrote in his address to the Sun-God—

" Verily under some name or other the whole world worships
  thee :
 All hail, true image of the Gods and of thy Father's face !
 The number six hundred and eight expressed by three
  letters,
 Forms thy Sacred Name, Surname, and Fateful Sign." [1]

Now what was this famous three-lettered name of the Sun-God. Are we acquainted with it, and, if so, why not acquainted with it as such ? Did the Christian Church, which propagated the

---

[1] Capella.

latest phase of Sun-God worship, and for centuries had all the manuscripts of the Roman World in its power, suppress both the name and its origin, or only the latter?

The name in question cannot have been Iao, for that was not a Greek name. Nor can it have been Iaou. It may be well to note, however, that Iaou or Jehovah, the name of the Sun-God, originally meant " He who causes (rain or lightning) to fall." [1] For the Greek word for Shower-giving, a term applied to the Sun-God, was of the required numerical value, six hundred and eight. And the word in question was a three-lettered one, $YH\Sigma$. It was the Sacred Name of the Sun-Gods Apollo and Bacchus. And the sacredness attached to this particular epithet of the Sun-God seems to have arisen from the fact that the letters transposed as $HY\Sigma$ signified Good.

Seeing, therefore, that $YH\Sigma$ was the Sacred Name of the Sun-God, his " nomen, cognomen, et omen," let us now inquire into the meaning

---

[1] *Encyc. Brit.*, "*Jehovah.*"

and origin of the I.H.S. of the Christian Church
displayed so prominently upon altars and elsewhere as the "nomen, cognomen, et omen"
of the Christ.

Some opponents of Christianity have traced
this I.H.S. to Iacchos, the mystic name of the
Sun-God Bacchus [1] and the Sun-God Dionysos.
But Christians laugh such explanations to scorn.
They have an explanation of their own.

Unfortunately, however, Christians have *several*
explanations of their I.H.S., and they cannot all
be true. And if some are false, perhaps all are
false. Let us examine them, and see.

Some Christians state quite positively that their
I.H.S. are the initial letters of the words "Jesus
Hominum Salvator." But a J is not an I; there
is no particular reason why the initial letters
of words signifying "Jesus the Saviour of men,"
rather than those of words signifying "Jesus
the Light of the World," etc., etc., should have
been chosen; there is no particular reason why
a Church whose documents were in Greek should

---

[1] Ar. Ran., Valck. *Hdt.*, 8, 65.

have chosen the initial letters of Latin words ; and no one can say who started the idea; nor can any Christian say when or why it was started.

Other Christians state just as positively that their I.H.S. are the initial letters of " In hoc signo," referring to the alleged vision by Constantine and his army of a cross of light in the sky with a motto attached to same. But that motto was in Greek, not Latin, and " In hoc signo " is simply a bad Latin translation— " In hoc signo vinces "—badly mutilated. There was nothing about "sign " in the original Greek, and the " vinces " has to be cut off and the " signo " invented before any I.H.S. can be discerned even in the Latin version of the motto in question.

Yet other Christians are equally positive that their I.H.S. are the first three letters of the Greek word *ΙΗΣΟΥΣ*, Jesus. But why immortalise half a name, to the disparagement of the other half? They cannot say.

Even the Jesuits, whose favourite device is this I.H.S. encircled with the rays of the Sun emanating from it, profess to be ignorant of any other origin than such self-evidently incorrect and mutually destructive ones as have been quoted as put forward by Christians.

And the fact that Christians differ among themselves as to the origin of their i.h.s., and can give no credible account of its origin, would, even if it stood by itself, be sufficient to justify the suspicion that the symbol i.h.s. they declare to be that of Jesus the Giver of Eternal Life, is either that of Iacchos the God of Eternal Youth, or the Sacred Name of the Sun-God already mentioned; and in any case, whether derived from Iacchos the mystic name of the Sun-God Bacchus, or from $\Upsilon H \Sigma$ the Sacred Name of the Sun-God whether called Bacchus or Apollo or by any appellation, is of Sun-God origin.

That Sun-God worship was, in the early days of our era, considered to be the basis of both Judaism and Christianity, may be gathered, among other sources, from the fact that Heliogabalus hoped to be able to unite all the inhabitants of Rome in the worship of the Emesne aerolite as an emblem of the Sun. Thus, as we read—

" Bringing together in his temple the Fire of Vesta, the Palladium, the Ancilia, and all the other most venerated relics ; and, moreover, the religion of the Jews and Samaritans, and the devotion of the Christians." [1]

As further connecting Mithraicism, Judaism, and Christianity, it may be pointed out that while forty days was the term of probation for those seeking to be initiated into the mysteries of the Persian Sun-God, this probation seems to be curiously reflected in the alleged forty years in the wilderness of the Israelites, the forty days in the wilderness of Jesus, the forty days between the alleged resurrection and ascension, and the forty days of Lent.

It is also noteworthy that the bread used in the ancient Mithraic Sacrament of the Eucharist was a round cake emblematic of the solar disc and therefore of life to come, the Sun-God being the Giver of Life. The wafer of the Christian Mass seems to have been copied from the Mithraic one, for some authorities derive the word Mass from

---

[1] Lampridius, 3.

"Mizd," the name given by the worshippers of Mithras to *their* " Host." [1]

As to the conventional portrait of Jesus, this is well known to be a direct descendant of representations of yet another conception of the Sun-God -- viz., Serapis.[2]

Now not only has Capella told us that in his time and before it the Egyptians worshipped the Sun-God not only as Osiris but also as Serapis (curiously enough he omits to mention Horus), but we further learn, from Macrobius, that—

"The City of Alexandria pays an almost frantic worship to Serapis and Isis ; nevertheless they show that all this veneration is merely offered to the Sun." [3]

While Vospiscus tells us that the well-informed Emperor Hadrian, in a letter to Servianus concerning the inhabitants of Alexandria, remarked that—

"Those who worship Serapis are likewise Chris-

---

[1] Seel.

[2] Rev. C. W. King, *Early Christian Numismatics*.

[3] Macrobius, i. 20.

tians; even those who style themselves the bishops of the Christ are devoted to Serapis."[1]

Moreover, it was doubtless as conceiving the Christ to be but another conception of the many-named Sun-God, that this same Emperor—who, having obtained entrance to the Mysteries of every religion in his world-wide empire, was of all men most likely to know—intended—

"To build a temple unto the Christ, and to rank Him in the number of the Gods."[2]

This intention of Hadrian was more than carried out by his successor Constantine, who, brought up to worship the Sun-God Apollo, choosing that God as his patron deity, recognising in the Christ or Logos another conception of the Sun-God, aware that he more or less owed his rise to supreme power to the enthusiastic backing he received from Christians, and seeing that the one thing the world-wide empire he re-united lacked was an equally world-wide religion, adopted the non-national and world-ramifying Christian faith,

---

[1] Vospiscus, *vit. Saturninus.*   [2] Lampridius, i. 43.

and made use of his power as Supreme Emperor
and Pontifex Maximus—High Priest of the Gods
of Rome—to dethrone the other Gods, destroy
their temples, and exalt the Christ in their stead,
making Christianity the State Religion of the
Roman Empire, and giving the Christian Church
powers and chances never before possessed by
any religious organisation.

Now religions never die ; they evolve, or merge,
into others.

Thus, owing to the action of an all-powerful
Emperor, was a Church established and a movement inaugurated which ultimately caused the
merging of the worship of many Sun-Gods into
that of one, and the elevation of the philosophic
conception of the Christ or Logos of God, throughout an almost world-wide empire, not as the deity
of this or that land or race, but as the one deity
common to all, the only Sun whether of Man's
physical or mental life, the *ratio* as well as the
oratio of the All-Father, the light within the soul
as well as the light without, a light intended to be
common to all, a catholic light, and therefore in
every sense the Light of the *World.*

CHAPTER X.

THE SUN-GOD OF PHILOSOPHY.

THE Church established and the movement inaugurated by Constantine, which caused the merging of the worship of many Sun-Gods into that of one, were, however, only established and inaugurated by him. Though their success was due to him, their being was not.

To whom, then, shall we attribute the first formation of Christianity ?

We cannot attribute the rise of Christianity to Jesus if we would pay due regard to reason and justice, for He did not preach belief in the Logos—*i.e.*, thought and speech—of the All-Father, and He expressly and repeatedly stated that His mission was to His fellow-countrymen only.

As a matter of fact, the three men chiefly

responsible for the birth of Christianity were Plato, Philo, and Paul.

Of this illustrious trio Plato may be said to have—in more senses than one—furnished the idea of, Philo to have provided the materials of, and Paul to have built, the fabric called Christianity.

Only the bare walls were built by Paul, however, their adornment being effected after his time. It should never be forgotten that the Christian Gospels were written after Paul preached to the nations a new and non-national creed. From his epistles it is quite clear that Paul had never heard of the now alleged miraculous birth of Jesus of a virgin, or of the proclamation of His birth by angels to shepherds, or of His miracles, or of His transfiguration or metamorphosis upon the mount, of His ascension to heaven in bodily form, or of many other marvels alleged concerning Jesus. These stories must therefore have been invented after Paul had passed away.

Christianity is, however, the result of the labours of Paul. Whence then did Paul obtain

the materials which he pieced together and so
zealously set forth as a new and non-national
faith ?

There is but one possible conclusion to any one
who consults the whole evidence with a well-
balanced mind—viz., that Paul drew his inspiration
from Philo.

What, too, more natural than that a Jew of
Paul's calibre and environment, a Roman citizen
brought up in a centre of Greek learning, should
have been influenced by the greatest of the
Jewish philosophers, and one who flourished in
yet another centre of Greek learning ?   However
uncultured Paul may have been, he could scarcely
fail to have heard of the fame of Philo.

Paul was born about the year A.C. 14,[1] at
Tarsus, a city in Cilicia which rivalled even
Athens and Alexandria as a centre of learning.[2]
He is said to have lived about fifty years, and to
have been martyred at Rome A.C. 64.

Philo was born at Alexandria about the year
20 B.C.   By some, however, he is said to have

---

[1] Schrader.   [2] Strabo, xiv. 5, 13.

been an old man when in A.C. 39-40 he was sent by the Jews of Alexandria to Rome, as an Ambassador, to the Emperor Caligula ; which would seem to indicate a somewhat earlier date.

As even the earliest date assignable to the earliest Epistle of Paul is A.C. 49-50, it is clear that Philo cannot have borrowed from Paul. And as Philo was born thirty or forty years before Paul, and, as can be seen from the size and number of his works, must have commenced writing at a comparatively early age, it is equally clear that, on the contrary, Paul could have borrowed from Philo.

Before discussing how much Paul borrowed from Philo, it is desirable that something should be said as to the meaning of the Greek word *Logos*, which repeatedly occurs in the works of Philo as signifying a well-known philosophic conception, and is several times used in that sense in the first chapter of the Gospel " according to " St. John.

The philosophic term in question is usually rendered into English as " the Word," and was a development of the " Idea " of Plato. As a translation, however, "the Word" is imperfect ; for Logos meant both Thought and Speech, both Reason and Manifestation. It was the first emanation from the All-Father, the Wisdom by which He created the heaven and the earth, the Sense which lurks in every wayside weed as well as in the poet's brain, the Reason which is the light of every sentient being, the Thought of the All-Father and the manifestation thereof, His first-born Son.

It was in this sense that the unknown author of the Gospel "according to" St. John, writing after Paul had passed away, declared that "In the beginning was the Logos, and the Logos was with God, and the Logos was God. The same was in the beginning with God. All things were made by Him ; and without Him was not anything made that was made" (John i. 1-3).

That Reason is here referred to by the author of the Gospel is clear, for he goes on to say : " In Him was "—*really*, " is "—" life ; and the life was the light of men " ; " That was the true Light, which lighteth every man that cometh into the world."

It is the Logos, which Jesus was alleged to
have been an incarnation of, that "lighteth every
man that cometh into the world." It is Reason
which is the Light of the World. The Son of
Mary and of Joseph ("Thy Father and I," Luke
ii. 49) does not light "every man which cometh
into the world," was not the light of the World
in the untold thousands of years ere Joseph and
Mary made each other's acquaintance, and is not
the Light of the World even to-day.

In this connection it may be mentioned that
not only does the newly discovered ancient copy
of the Gospel openly state that Jesus was the
Son of Joseph the carpenter, and make no
mystery about it whatever, and not only does
even the Authorised Version of the Gospel
"according to" St. Luke represent Mary—who
ought to have known—as speaking to Jesus of
His father Joseph (Luke ii. 48), but what is
rendered in our English Bibles as " And Joseph
and His mother marvelled at those things which
were spoken of Him " (Luke ii. 33), reads, " And
His father and His mother marvelled " in the
original text of the *Codex Bezæ*, the *Codex*

Sinaiticus, and the *Codex Vaticanus—i.e.,* in the oldest copies extant.

Bearing these facts in mind, let us now turn to the works of Philo, the famous Jewish philosopher who wrote during and after the lifetime of Jesus, but had evidently never heard of the marvels recorded in the Gospels composed by the followers of his exploiter Paul of Tarsus.

In one passage Philo writes—

"Why, as though speaking of another God, does he say 'I made Man in the image of God,' but not in his own image? The answer is, that nothing mortal could be made like the supreme All-Father, but only like the Second God, the Word. For the rational impress in the soul of man must be stamped by divine Reason, and cannot have as its archetype God who is above Reason." [1]

Here we see the all-significant fact that long before such doctrines were preached to the world as a non-national religion by Paul and his followers, both the deity of the Idea, Reason, or Word of the All-Father, and the occupation by

---

[1] *Frag.* ii. 625.

same of the second place, were set forth by this famous Jewish philosopher.

In another place Philo writes—

"God is the most generic thing, and the Word of God is second." [1]

Here again, it will be noted, emphasis is laid upon the assertion that the Logos held the second place among the Powers of the Universe.

The belief of Christians that though all things necessarily owe their origin to the All-Father, it was the Word " by whom all things were made," is also clearly traceable to Philo, who remarks :—

" The Word, by which the world was made, is the Image of the Supreme Deity." [2]

In this passage can also be seen the origin of the declaration in the Epistle to the Hebrews, that the Christ or Word was the "express image " of the All-Father.

---

[1] *Leg All.* ii. 21 (i. 82).

[2] *De Monarchia*, II. ii. 225.

In another of the works of Philo we come across the sentence—

"God sealed the entire Cosmos with an Image and Idea, his own Word." [1]

The significance of this passage is too self-evident to need pointing out.

Yet another noteworthy saying of Philo is the one which runs as follows—

"As those who are unable to gaze upon the Sun, look upon his reflected radiance as a Sun, so likewise the Image of God, his angel Word, is himself considered to be God." [2]

Here the Logos is not only once more stated to be, though an emanation from the All-Father, considered God, but is also, as was the Sun-God Apollo, compared to the Light issuing from that central Fire, of which, according to the *Magic Oracles*, "All things are the offspring." [3]

We also meet with the expression—

---

[1] *Somn.* ii. 6 ; i. 665.
[2] *De Somn.*, i. 40, 41.
[3] Porphyry, *de Autro Nympharum.*

" The *Shepherd* of his holy flock." [1]

The connection in which the term is used is noteworthy.

Still more significant than the foregoing is the following passage—

" That High Priest, the holy Word, the First-born of God." [2]

The fact that this was how a philosopher of the previous generation wrote and thought, shows where Paul derived his inspiration from.

In another of the works of Philo we come across the sentence—

" His Word, which is his Interpreter." [3]

This description of the Logos as the Interpreter or Mediator between God and Man, is also significant.

Elsewhere we come across the sentence—

" In the likeness of Man." [4]

---

[1] *De Agric.*, i. 308.
[2] *De Somnis*, i. 653.
[3] *De Legis Allegor.*, iii. 73.
[4] *De Confu. Ling.*, i. 427.

The expression and idea are now considered Christian, though of pre-Christian origin.

A most important passage next claims our attention—

" His first-begotten Son." [1]

Here Philo once more distinctly calls the Logos or Word the first-begotten Son of the All-Father. This is the very idea afterwards so enlarged upon by Paul, and in yet later times adopted by the author of the Gospel "according to " St. John.

In another of Philo's works we read—

" To his Word, the chief and most ancient of all in heaven, the great Author of the Universe gave this especial gift, that he should stand as an *Intercessor* between the Creator and the created." [2]

The works of Philo were thus the source whence Paul derived the most prominent of the thoughts which distinguished his teaching. How then can Paul be said to have been inspired of

---

[1] *De Agric.*, i. 308.
[2] *Quis Rerum Divin. Hæres.*, i. 501.

God if Philo thought God's thought before him ?
The fact that Paul claimed, as bestowed in favour
to himself by God, that which he had borrowed
without acknowledgment from Man, shows that
Paul had a failing common to the majority of
enthusiasts, that of acting upon the principle that
the end justifies the means.

In yet another sentence of Philo's we have the
remark—

" And the Word is, accordingly, the Advocate for
all Mortals." [1]

As Philo had thus laid it down that the conception of Plato and other Greek philosophers
known as the Idea of God, or Logos of God, or
Word, was the Second God, the first-begotten
Son of the All-Father, the divinely appointed
Intercessor for the created, and the Advocate
with the Father, long before Paul or any other
Christian made use of the same ideas, the conclusion is obvious.

Another passage of Philo's runs as follows—

---

[1] *Quis Rerum Divin. Hæres.*, i. 502.

" The same Word is the Intercessor for Man, who
is always tending to corruption ; and the Word is also
the appointed Messenger of God, the governor of all
things, to Man in subjection to him." [1]

Here again we see ideas afterwards adopted by
Paul and his followers without acknowledgment
of their true source.

Note, too, the following remarkable pronounce-
ment by the great Jewish Philosopher born before
our era whose works we are considering—

" What man is there of true judgment who, when
he sees the deeds of most men, is not ready to call
out aloud to God, the great Saviour, that he would
be pleased to take off this load of sin, and, *by
appointing a price and ransom for the soul*, restore it
to its original liberty." [2]

Who would think from the orations of
Christian preachers that this idea of God
appointing a price and ransom for the soul, was
a pre-Christian—and therefore non-Christian—
one ?

[1] *Quis Rerum Divin. Hæres.*, i. 501.
[2] *De Confus. Ling.*, i. 418.

Elsewhere in the works of Philo we find the following ever-to-be-remembered lines, written, be it borne in mind, possibly as early as the childhood of Jesus, and in any case long before the Epistles of Paul—much less the other books of the New Testament—were written —

" He therefore exhorts every person who is able to exert himself in the race which he is to run, to bend his course without remission to the divine Word above, who is the fountain of all wisdom, that, by drinking of this sacred spring, he, instead of death, may receive the reward of everlasting life." [1]

To repeat a former inquiry, who would imagine from the pronouncements of Christian preachers that such essentially Christian ideas as these were in reality pre-Christian, and, so far as origin is concerned, therefore non-Christian ?

Another notable passage to be found in the works of the great Jewish philosopher is the following —

" The Eternal Word of the Eternal God is the

---

[1] *De Profugis*, i. 560, 31.

sure and fixed foundation upon which all things depend." [1]

Many echoes of this idea are to be found in the Epistles of Paul and the Gospels and other Epistles afterwards written by his followers.

In another passage Philo refers to the Word of the Father as—

" Being the Image of God and the First-born of all intelligent creatures, he is seated immediately next to the One God without any interval of separation." [2]

This short sentence contains no less than three ideas afterwards set forth by Paul and his followers as inspired.

Elsewhere in the same work Philo wrote—

" We maintain that by the High Priest is meant the Word, who is free from all voluntary and involuntary transgressions, being of heavenly parentage." [3]

In other words, a lamb " without blemish and without spot "; the Lamb of God.

---

[1] *De Plantatione Noe,* i. 331.
[2] *De Profugis,* i. 561, 16.
[3] *Ibid.,* i. 562, 13.

In another place we find Philo declaring that—

"The Word of God is the *Physician* and *Healer* of all our evils." [1]

This idea also was adopted by Paul and his followers.

Philo also tells us that—

"Even if no one is as yet worthy to be called a son of God, one should nevertheless labour earnestly to be adorned like unto his First-born Son the Word, who is the eldest of the Angels, the great Archangel with many names, and is called the Authority, the Name of God, the Word, the Image of Man, and the Guardian of Israel." [2]

Who would think to hear the exhortations of Christian preachers that one should strive to be like unto the Word which was in the beginning with God and which was God, that after all the idea is a pre-Christian one?

Elsewhere we read that—

---

[1] *De Leg. Alleg.*, i. 122, 17.
[2] *De Confu. Ling*, i. 427.

"God, by the same Word by whom He made all things, will raise the good man from the dregs of this world and exalt him near unto himself." [1]

Here again we find an idea set forth by Paul and his followers as inspired, but in reality of pre-Christian origin.

In another work we read—

"The Deity acts with the most consummate order and rectitude, and has appointed His First-born, the upright Word, like the lieutenant of a mighty prince, to take the care of His sacred flock." [2]

Nor is this the only passage where Philo distinctly describes the Word or Son of God as the Shepherd of God's flock. It is therefore no wonder that we find him so described in the Epistles and Gospels.

The five following quotations all refer to the same idea as each other—

"Man lifts his eyes to heaven and beholds the manna, which is a type of the Word, and affords

---

[1] *De Sacrificis* i., 165. 5.   [2] *De Agric.*, i. 308, 27.

heavenly and immortal nutriment to the intelligent soul."[1]

"The heavenly food he elsewhere calls manna, the same figuratively as the First of all Beings, the Divine Word."[2]

"The heavenly food of the soul, called manna, is distributed equally to all who will make a good use of it, by the holy and divine Word."[3]

"Do you then see what is meant by this nutriment of the soul, manna? Even the never-failing Word."[4]

"This is the Bread, that nourishment which God appointed to be applied to the soul of Man, the Word."[5]

Now who again would think, to hear Christians expatiating upon the contents of the New Testament, that the idea therein set forth that the Word was the Bread of Life which came down from heaven, was a pre-Christian idea? Yet, as has been shown, it appears as a full-fledged philosophic conception in the works of a man

---

[1] *Quis Rer. Divin. Hær.*, i. 484, 3.
[2] *De Deter. Potiori Infid.*, i. 213, 45.
[3] *Quis Rer. Divin. Hær.*, i. 499, 44.
[4] *De Leg. Alleg.*, i. 120, 34.
[5] *Ibid.*, i. 121, 26.

who was born a generation before Jesus, seventy years or so before Paul wrote his first Epistle, and still longer before the followers of Paul compiled the Gospels, which are so full of accounts of alleged marvels of which Paul was evidently ignorant.

Even the Christian doctrine of a Trinity, that, except in a forged passage—which, though still in the Authorised Version of the Bible, is omitted from the Revised Version—is unmentioned in any of the writings forming the collection known as the New Testament, may as an idea have been derived from Philo. For we find that famous philosopher writing—

" God, escorted on each side by Personages from on high whose attributes were Goodness and Power, the Divinity in the middle being in union with the other two, impressed a Threefold appearance upon the soul of Abraham who beheld them." [1]

And, as a philosophic conception, the Trinity was of very early date, for perhaps the greatest

---

[1] *De Sacrificis*, i. 173, 12.

of the Greek philosophers declared centuries before our era that—

"Three or the Triad is the first of unequals, it is the number containing the most sublime mysteries, it represents (1) God; (2) the Soul of the Universe; (3) the Spirit of Man." [1]

And concerning a famous sage who lived at a yet earlier period, Plutarch tells us that—

"Zoroaster is said to have made a Threefold distribution of things, and to have assigned the first and highest rank to Ormazd, who in the Oracles is called The Father, . . . and the middle to Mithras, who in the same Oracles is called the Second Mind." [2]

It is therefore clear that long before Jesus was born the Trinity existed as a philosophic conception. Also that the second place in the trinity of Gods, or triune nature of God, was given indifferently to the Word and the Sun-God, these being regarded as more or less identical.

In various parts of the works of Philo we come across such remarks as—

---

[1] Pythagoras   [2] *De Iside et Osiride*, 370

" There are two temples of God, one of which is this world, and the other is the rational soul." [1]

"The Deity could never find a more excellent temple than the rational part of Man." [2]

The famous saying that God dwelleth not in "temples made with hands," is evidently traceable to this source.

Even the extraordinary assertion of Paul and his followers that no amount of virtue is in itself sufficient to assure one's salvation, seems to have been derived from Philo.   For he wrote,—

" The only sure and well-founded blessing to which we can trust is Faith." [3]

"Virtue without God's sanction can never profit us." [4]

And the assertions of priests that, no matter how vile one's past life, faith in their creed can save, and no matter how unselfish one's past life, want of faith will damn, can easily be supported by other such passages in the works of the great Jewish philosopher.

---

[1] *De Somniis*, i., 653, 22.   [3] *De Abrahamo*, ii. 38.

[2] *De Nobilitate*, ii. 437, 11.   [4] *De Deteriore-infidiando*, i. 203.

Elsewhere in the works of Philo are to be found the following passages—

" The Image of God is his eternal Word." [1]
" This High Priest is the holy and divine Word, who is not capable either of voluntary or of involuntary sin. Hence his head is anointed (Christos)." [2]

Much of the contents of the Epistles of Paul and the Gospels of his followers can be traced to such passages as these. And the fact that our " Christ" is but an evolution of the Greek word for "anointed," the past tense of the verb *chrio*, to smear over or anoint, is noteworthy in this connection.

Even the theory that " we shall be like Him, for we shall see Him as He is," was evidently derived by Paul and his followers from Philo. For that philosopher wrote,—

" Such persons shall find pardon from the Saviour and Merciful God, and receive a most choice and noble advantage in being made like unto the divine Word." [3]

---

[1] *De Confu. Ling.*, i. 427.   [2] *De Somniis*, i. 653.
[3] *De Execrationibus*, ii. 435.

And the well-known passages in Phil. iii. 21 and
1 John iii. 2 are clearly inspired by the foregoing
conception.

As to the terms which this philosopher used
in speaking of the pre-Christian conception of
the Logos or Word, the Christos or Anointed,
we have seen that Philo called him the great
" High Priest," the " Second God," the good
" Shepherd," the " Image of God," the " Interpreter " of God to Man, God's " First-begotten
Son," the " Intercessor " between the Creator
and the created, the "Advocate " with the Father,
the "Giver of the Water of Everlasting Life," the
" Foundation of the Universe," " Seated next to
God the Father," the " Sinless One," the " Bread
of Life," and the "Physician and Healer of Souls."
Elsewhere he calls the Logos or Christos, the
"Word" or "Christ,"—

" The Intellectual Sun." [1]
" The Light of the World." [2]
" The Substitute of God." [3]
" His Beloved Son." [4]

[1] *De Somniis*, i. 6, 414, 632-3.   [3] *De Leg. Alleg.*, i. 129, 4.
[2] *Ibid.*, i. 6, 414, 632-3.   [4] *De Somniis*, i. 656, 48.

What then have we in pre-Christian philosophy but Christianity in formation ? What is Christianity but a new and allegorical representation of old and philosophical ideas ?

Even the absolute necessity, not only of faith in the All-Father, but also of faith in His Beloved Son the Word, who was " In the beginning," who was "with God," and who "was God," was insisted upon by Philo the Philosopher long before it was preached by his exploiter Paul, the founder of Christianity. For this pre-Christian writer, Philo Judæus of Alexandria, explicitly laid it down that—

" It is necessary for a person performing his duty to the All-Father to apply to His Son, as to an Advocate the most perfect in every virtue, both to have his sins forgiven, and also for the obtaining of every good gift." [1]

And this thought is the very essence of the non-national religion afterwards preached, and called Christianity.

It is therefore clear that, while the spread of

---

[1] *De Execrationibus*, ii. 435, 29.

Christianity was due to its being a non-national creed, and one whose propagators for ever undercut all possible competitors (offering those who had lived the vilest of lives, eternal bliss in return for mere faith ; even asserting such faith to be just as effectual when not yielded until one was dying as when yielded in one's prime and followed by years of self-sacrifice), and its ultimate triumph to the fact that Constantine made it the State-Religion of the Roman Empire, its origin was due to the preaching to the ignorant masses of many nations the ideas of the philosophers wrapped up in what may be likened to an instructive nursery tale, the hero of which, however real in himself, was the imaginary incarnation or personification of the Sun-God—a personification, that is, of the intellectual Sun conceived by the intellectual few, as well as of the physical Sun adored by the unintellectual many.

IMPRIMATUR :

J. D. P.

1895 : 1 : 21.

ALSO AVAILABLE FROM THE BOOK TREE

Babylonian Influence on the Bible and Popular Beliefs: A Comparative Study of Genesis I.2, by A. Smythe Palmer. ISBN 1-58509-000-X • 124 pages • 6 x 9 • trade paper • $12.95

Biography of Satan: Exposing the Origins of the Devil, by Kersey Graves. ISBN 1-885395-11-6 • 168 pages • 5 1/2 x 8 1/2 • trade paper • $13.95

The Malleus Maleficarum: The Notorious Handbook Once Used to Condemn and Punish "Witches", by Heinrich Kramer and James Sprenger. ISBN 1-58509-098-0 • 332 pages • 6 x 9 • trade paper • $25.95

Crux Ansata: An Indictment of the Roman Catholic Church, by H. G. Wells. ISBN 1-58509-210-X • 160 pages • 6 x 9 • trade paper • $14.95

Emanuel Swedenborg: The Spiritual Columbus, by U.S.E. (William Spear). ISBN 1-58509-096-4 • 208 pages • 6 x 9 • trade paper • $17.95

Dragons and Dragon Lore, by Ernest Ingersoll. ISBN 1-58509-021-2 • 228 pages • 6 x 9 • trade paper • illustrated • $17.95

The Vision of God, by Nicholas of Cusa. ISBN 1-58509-004-2 • 160 pages • 5 x 8 • trade paper • $13.95

The Historical Jesus and the Mythical Christ: Separating Fact From Fiction, by Gerald Massey. ISBN 1-58509-073-5 • 244 pages • 6 x 9 • trade paper • $18.95

Gog and Magog: The Giants in Guildhall; Their Real and Legendary History, with an Account of Other Giants at Home and Abroad, by F.W. Fairholt. ISBN 1-58509-084-0 • 172 pages • 6 x 9 • trade paper • $16.95

The Origin and Evolution of Religion, by Albert Churchward. ISBN 1-58509-078-6 • 504 pages • 6 x 9 • trade paper • $39.95

The Origin of Biblical Traditions, by Albert T. Clay. ISBN 1-58509-065-4 • 220 pages • 5 1/2 x 8 1/2 • trade paper • $17.95

Aryan Sun Myths, by Sarah Elizabeth Titcomb, Introduction by Charles Morris. ISBN 1-58509-069-7 • 192 pages • 6 x 9 • trade paper • $15.95

The Social Record of Christianity, by Joseph McCabe. Includes *The Lies and Fallacies of the Encyclopedia Britannica*, ISBN 1-58509-215-0 • 204 pages • 6 x 9 • trade paper • $17.95

The History of the Christian Religion and Church During the First Three Centuries, by Dr. Augustus Neander. ISBN 1-58509-077-8 • 112 pages • 6 x 9 • trade paper • $12.95

Ancient Symbol Worship: Influence of the Phallic Idea in the Religions of Antiquity, by Hodder M. Westropp and C. Staniland Wake. ISBN 1-58509-048-4 • 120 pages • 6 x 9 • trade paper • illustrated • $12.95

The Gnosis: Or Ancient Wisdom in the Christian Scriptures, by William Kingsland. ISBN 1-58509-047-6 • 232 pages • 6 x 9 • trade paper • $18.95

The Evolution of the Idea of God: An Inquiry into the Origin of Religions, by Grant Allen. ISBN 1-58509-074-3 • 160 pages • 6 x 9 • trade paper • $14.95

Sun Lore of All Ages: A Survey of Solar Mythology, Folklore, Customs, Worship, Festivals, and Superstition, by William Tyler Olcott. ISBN 1-58509-044-1 • 316 pages • 6 x 9 • trade paper • $24.95

Nature Worship: An Account of Phallic Faiths and Practices Ancient and Modern, by the Author of Phallicism with an Introduction by Tedd St. Rain. ISBN 1-58509-049-2 • 112 pages • 6 x 9 • trade paper • illustrated • $12.95

Life and Religion, by Max Muller. ISBN 1-885395-10-8 • 237 pages • 5 1/2 x 8 1/2 • trade paper • $14.95

Jesus: God, Man, or Myth? An Examination of the Evidence, by Herbert Cutner. ISBN 1-58509-072-7 • 304 pages • 6 x 9 • trade paper • $23.95

Pagan and Christian Creeds: Their Origin and Meaning, by Edward Carpenter. ISBN 1-58509-024-7 • 316 pages • 5 1/2 x 8 1/2 • trade paper • $24.95

The Christ Myth: A Study, by Elizabeth Evans. ISBN 1-58509-037-9 • 136 pages • 6 x 9 • trade paper • $13.95

Popery: Foe of the Church and the Republic, by Joseph F. Van Dyke. ISBN 1-58509-058-1 • 336 pages • 6 x 9 • trade paper • illustrated • $25.95

Career of Religious Ideas, by Hudson Tuttle. ISBN 1-58509-066-2 • 172 pages • 5 x 8 • trade paper • $15.95

Buddhist Suttas: Major Scriptural Writings from Early Buddhism, by T.W, Rhys Davids. ISBN 1-58509-079-4 • 376 pages • 6 x 9 • trade paper • $27.95

Early Buddhism, by T. W. Rhys Davids, Includes *Buddhist Ethics: The Way to Salvation?*, by Paul Tice. ISBN 1-58509-076-X • 112 pages • 6 x 9 • trade paper • $12.95

The Fountain-Head of Religion: A Comparative Study of the Principal Religions of the World and a Manifestation of their Common Origin from the Vedas, by Ganga Prasad. ISBN 1-58509-054-9 • 276 pages • 6 x 9 • trade paper • $22.95

India: What Can It Teach Us?, by Max Muller. ISBN 1-58509-064-6 • 284 pages • 5 1/2 x 8 1/2 • trade paper • $22.95

Matrix of Power: How the World has Been Controlled by Powerful People Without Your Knowledge, by Jordan Maxwell. ISBN 1-58509-120-0 • 104 pages • 6 x 9 • trade paper • $12.95

Cyberculture Counterconspiracy: A Steamshovel Web Reader, Volume One, edited by Kenn Thomas. ISBN 1-58509-125-1 • 180 pages • 6 x 9 • trade paper • illustrated • $16.95

Cyberculture Counterconspiracy: A Steamshovel Web Reader, Volume Two, edited by Kenn Thomas. ISBN 1-58509-126-X • 132 pages • 6 x 9 • trade paper • illustrated • $13.95

Oklahoma City Bombing: The Suppressed Truth, by Jon Rappoport. ISBN 1-885395-22-1 • 112 pages • 5 1/2 x 8 1/2 • trade paper • $12.95

The Protocols of the Learned Elders of Zion, by Victor Marsden. ISBN 1-58509-015-8 • 312 pages • 6 x 9 • trade paper • $24.95

Secret Societies and Subversive Movements, by Nesta H. Webster. ISBN 1-58509-092-1 • 432 pages • 6 x 9 • trade paper • $29.95

The Secret Doctrine of the Rosicrucians, by Magus Incognito. ISBN 1-58509-091-3 • 256 pages • 6 x 9 • trade paper • $20.95

The Origin and Evolution of Freemasonry: Connected with the Origin and Evolution of the Human Race, by Albert Churchward. ISBN 1-58509-029-8 • 240 pages • 6 x 9 • trade paper • $18.95

The Lost Key: An Explanation and Application of Masonic Symbols, by Prentiss Tucker. ISBN 1-58509-050-6 • 192 pages • 6 x 9 • trade paper • illustrated • $15.95

The Character, Claims, and Practical Workings of Freemasonry, by Rev. C.G. Finney. ISBN 1-58509-094-8 • 288 pages • 6 x 9 • trade paper • $22.95

The Secret World Government or "The Hidden Hand": The Unrevealed in History, by Maj.-Gen., Count Cherep-Spiridovich. ISBN 1-58509-093-X • 270 pages • 6 x 9 • trade paper • $21.95

The Magus, Book One: A Complete System of Occult Philosophy, by Francis Barrett. ISBN 1-58509-031-X • 200 pages • 6 x 9 • trade paper • illustrated • $16.95

The Magus, Book Two: A Complete System of Occult Philosophy, by Francis Barrett. ISBN 1-58509-032-8 • 220 pages • 6 x 9 • trade paper • illustrated • $17.95

The Magus, Book One and Two: A Complete System of Occult Philosophy, by Francis Barrett. ISBN 1-58509-033-6 • 420 pages • 6 x 9 • trade paper • illustrated • $34.90

The Key of Solomon The King, by S. Liddell MacGregor Mathers. ISBN 1-58509-022-0 • 152 pages • 6 x 9 • trade paper • illustrated • $12.95

Magic and Mystery in Tibet, by Alexandra David-Neel. ISBN 1-58509-097-2 • 352 pages • 6 x 9 • trade paper • $26.95

The Comte de St. Germain, by I. Cooper Oakley. ISBN 1-58509-068-9 • 280 pages • 6 x 9 • trade paper • illustrated • $22.95

Alchemy Rediscovered and Restored, by A. Cockren. ISBN 1-58509-028-X • 156 pages • 5 1/2 x 8 1/2 • trade paper • $13.95

The 6th and 7th Books of Moses, with an Introduction by Paul Tice. ISBN 1-58509-045-X • 188 pages • 6 x 9 • trade paper • illustrated • $16.95

Of Heaven and Earth: Essays Presented at the First Sitchin Studies Day, edited by Zecharia Sitchin. ISBN 1-885395-17-5 • 164 pages • 5 1/2 x 8 1/2 • trade paper • illustrated • $14.95

God Games: What Do You Do Forever?, by Neil Freer. ISBN 1-885395-39-6 • 312 pages • 6 x 9 • trade paper • $19.95

Space Travelers and the Genesis of the Human Form: Evidence of Intelligent Contact in the Solar System, by Joan d'Arc. ISBN 1-58509-127-8 • 208 pages • 6 x 9 • trade paper • illustrated • $18.95

Humanity's Extraterrestrial Origins: ET Influences on Humankind's Biological and Cultural Evolution, by Dr. Arthur David Horn with Lynette Mallory-Horn. ISBN 3-931652-31-9 • 373 pages • 6 x 9 • trade paper • $17.00

Past Shock: The Origin of Religion and Its Impact on the Human Soul, by Jack Barranger. ISBN 1-885395-08-6 • 126 pages • 6 x 9 • trade paper • illustrated • $12.95

Flying Serpents and Dragons: The Story of Mankind's Reptilian Past, by R.A. Boulay. ISBN 1-885395-38-8 • 276 pages • 6 x 9 • trade paper • illustrated • $19.95

Triumph of the Human Spirit: The Greatest Achievements of the Human Soul and How Its Power Can Change Your Life, by Paul Tice. ISBN 1-885395-57-4 • 295 pages • 6 x 9 • trade paper • illustrated • $19.95

Mysteries Explored: The Search for Human Origins, UFOs, and Religious Beginnings, by Jack Barranger and Paul Tice. ISBN 1-58509-101-4 • 104 pages • 6 x 9 • trade paper • $12.95

Mushrooms and Mankind: The Impact of Mushrooms on Human Consciousness and Religion, by James Arthur. ISBN 1-58509-151-0 • 103 pages • 6 x 9 • trade paper • $12.95

Vril or Vital Magnetism, with an Introduction by Paul Tice. ISBN 1-58509-030-1 • 124 pages • 5 1/2 x 8 1/2 • trade paper • $12.95

The Odic Force: Letters on Od and Magnetism, by Karl von Reichenbach. ISBN 1-58509-001-8 • 192 pages • 6 x 9 • trade paper • $15.95

The New Revelation: The Coming of a New Spiritual Paradigm, by Arthur Conan Doyle. ISBN 1-58509-220-7 • 124 pages • 6 x 9 • trade paper • $12.95

The Astral World: Its Scenes, Dwellers, and Phenomena, by Swami Panchadasi. ISBN 1-58509-071-9 • 104 pages • 6 x 9 • trade paper • $11.95

Reason and Belief: The Impact of Scientific Discovery on Religious and Spiritual Faith, by Sir Oliver Lodge. ISBN 1-58509-226-6 • 180 pages • 6 x 9 • trade paper • $17.95

William Blake: A Biography, by Basil De Selincourt. ISBN 1-58509-225-8 • 384 pages • 6 x 9 • trade paper • $28.95

The Divine Pymander: And Other Writings of Hermes Trismegistus, translated by John D. Chambers. ISBN 1-58509-046-8 • 196 pages • 6 x 9 • trade paper • $16.95

Theosophy and The Secret Doctrine, by Harriet L. Henderson. Includes *H.P. Blavatsky: An Outline of Her Life*, by Herbert Whyte. ISBN 1-58509-075-1 • 132 pages • 6 x 9 • trade paper • $13.95

The Light of Egypt, Volume One: The Science of the Soul and the Stars, by Thomas H. Burgoyne. ISBN 1-58509-051-4 • 320 pages • 6 x 9 • trade paper • illustrated • $24.95

The Light of Egypt, Volume Two: The Science of the Soul and the Stars, by Thomas H. Burgoyne. ISBN 1-58509-052-2 • 224 pages • 6 x 9 • trade paper • illustrated • $17.95

The Jumping Frog and 18 Other Stories: 19 Unforgettable Mark Twain Stories, by Mark Twain. ISBN 1-58509-200-2 • 128 pages • 6 x 9 • trade paper • $12.95

The Devil's Dictionary: A Guidebook for Cynics, by Ambrose Bierce. ISBN 1-58509-016-6 • 144 pages • 6 x 9 • trade paper • $12.95

The Smoky God: Or The Voyage to the Inner World, by Willis George Emerson. ISBN 1-58509-067-0 • 184 pages • 6 x 9 • trade paper • illustrated • $15.95

A Short History of the World, by H.G. Wells. ISBN 1-58509-211-8 • 320 pages • 6 x 9 • trade paper • $24.95

The Voyages and Discoveries of the Companions of Columbus, by Washington Irving. ISBN 1-58509-500-1 • 352 pages • 6 x 9 • hard cover • $39.95

History of Baalbek, by Michel Alouf. ISBN 1-58509-063-8 • 196 pages • 5 x 8 • trade paper • illustrated • $15.95

Ancient Egyptian Masonry: The Building Craft, by Sommers Clarke and R. Engelback. ISBN 1-58509-059-X • 350 pages • 6 x 9 • trade paper • illustrated • $26.95

That Old Time Religion: The Story of Religious Foundations, by Jordan Maxwell and Paul Tice. ISBN 1-58509-100-6 • 103 pages • 6 x 9 • trade paper • $12.95

The Book of Enoch: A Work of Visionary Revelation and Prophecy, Revealing Divine Secrets and Fantastic Information about Creation, Salvation, Heaven and Hell, translated by R. H. Charles. ISBN 1-58509-019-0 • 152 pages • 5 1/2 x 8 1/2 • trade paper • $13.95

The Book of Enoch: Translated from the Editor's Ethiopic Text and Edited with an Enlarged Introduction, Notes and Indexes, Together with a Reprint of the Greek Fragments, edited by R. H. Charles. ISBN 1-58509-080-8 • 448 pages • 6 x 9 • trade paper • $34.95

The Book of the Secrets of Enoch, translated from the Slavonic by W. R. Morfill. Edited, with Introduction and Notes by R. H. Charles. ISBN 1-58509-020-4 • 148 pages • 5 1/2 x 8 1/2 • trade paper • $13.95

Enuma Elish: The Seven Tablets of Creation, Volume One, by L. W. King. ISBN 1-58509-041-7 • 236 pages • 6 x 9 • trade paper • illustrated • $18.95

Enuma Elish: The Seven Tablets of Creation, Volume Two, by L. W. King. ISBN 1-58509-042-5 • 260 pages • 6 x 9 • trade paper • illustrated • $19.95

Enuma Elish, Volumes One and Two: The Seven Tablets of Creation, by L. W. King. Two volumes from above bound as one. ISBN 1-58509-043-3 • 496 pages • 6 x 9 • trade paper • illustrated • $38.90

The Archko Volume: Documents that Claim Proof to the Life, Death, and Resurrection of Christ, by Drs. McIntosh and Twyman. ISBN 1-58509-082-4 • 248 pages • 6 x 9 • trade paper • $20.95

The Lost Language of Symbolism: An Inquiry into the Origin of Certain Letters, Words, Names, Fairy-Tales, Folklore, and Mythologies, by Harold Bayley. ISBN 1-58509-070-0 • 384 pages • 6 x 9 • trade paper • $27.95

The Book of Jasher: A Suppressed Book that was Removed from the Bible, Referred to in Joshua and Second Samuel, translated by Albinus Alcuin (800 AD). ISBN 1-58509-081-6 • 304 pages • 6 x 9 • trade paper • $24.95

The Bible's Most Embarrassing Moments, with an Introduction by Paul Tice. ISBN 1-58509-025-5 • 172 pages • 5 x 8 • trade paper • $14.95

History of the Cross: The Pagan Origin and Idolatrous Adoption and Worship of the Image, by Henry Dana Ward. ISBN 1-58509-056-5 • 104 pages • 6 x 9 • trade paper • illustrated • $11.95

Was Jesus Influenced by Buddhism? A Comparative Study of the Lives and Thoughts of Gautama and Jesus, by Dwight Goddard. ISBN 1-58509-027-1 • 252 pages • 6 x 9 • trade paper • $19.95

History of the Christian Religion to the Year Two Hundred, by Charles B. Waite. ISBN 1-885395-15-9 • 556 pages • 6 x 9 • hard cover • $25.00

Symbols, Sex, and the Stars, by Ernest Busenbark. ISBN 1-885395-19-1 • 396 pages • 5 1/2 x 8 1/2 • trade paper • $22.95

History of the First Council of Nice: A World's Christian Convention, A.D. 325, by Dean Dudley. ISBN 1-58509-023-9 • 132 pages • 5 1/2 x 8 1/2 • trade paper • $12.95

The World's Sixteen Crucified Saviors, by Kersey Graves. ISBN 1-58509-018-2 • 436 pages • 5 1/2 x 8 1/2 • trade paper • $29.95

www.ingramcontent.com/pod-product-compliance
Lightning Source LLC
Chambersburg PA
CBHW070349090426
42733CB00009B/1347